peterandre

ALL ABOUT US –
MY STORY

i

peterandre
ALL ABOUT US –
MY STORY

JOHN BLAKE

Published by John Blake Publishing Ltd,
3 Bramber Court, 2 Bramber Road,
London W14 9PB, England

www.johnblakepublishing.co.uk

www.facebook.com/Johnblakepub 🔳
twitter.com/johnblakepub 🔳

First published in paperback in 2007

ISBN: 978-1-84454-918-4

British Library Cataloguing-in-Publication Data:

A catalogue record for this book is available from the British Library.

Design by www.envydesign.co.uk

Printed in Great Britain by CPI Group (UK) Ltd

Papers used by John Blake Publishing are natural, recyclable products
made from wood grown in sustainable forests. The manufacturing processes
conform to the environmental regulations of the country of origin.

For Harvey and Junior

ACKNOWLEDGEMENTS

TO MY WONDERFUL wife, Kate, and two beautiful children, Harvey and Junior – you are my life.

To my mother Thea and my father Savva, thank you for being the most supportive and loving parents in the last 33 years. I am a lucky son.

My brothers and sister, Andrew, Chris, Danny, Michael and Debbie – we have seen the world together. We have had the best laughs, we've been through hell together – now hurry up and all get married so that we can share our families together. A special thanks to my bro Chris for believing in me since the beginning.

To Kate's wonderful family – Amy, Paul, Sophie, Daniel and Louise – thanks for welcoming me into your family. A special thank you to Amy for her incredible help with our Harvey, you truly are a wonder woman.

My best friend George Nicolaou – anyone who reads this book will understand why you are the best friend that anyone could ask for. Thanks for being my best man.

My number two man and brilliant friend, Reno Nicastro – café? Let's take on the world, brother.

Thanks to my good friend Angelo Panayiotou and his family for being there for me during the low times, when I really needed someone.

I would also like to thank my management team – Claire Powell, Neville Hendricks, Nicola Partridge and everyone else who has worked with them or does work with them through my career. Claire, I especially thank you, as you believed in me from day one twelve years ago. How much have we been through? I love you so much as a friend as well as a manager.

A special thank you to Maggie Hanbury, for all her help with the book and for her belief in me.

To Richard and Janet Desmond and all the Express group, thank you for being a major part of my new life. Kate might want a learjet, I just want continued success as friends and in business.

My great friends Gary and Phil, you guys really are true friends. Starbucks?

To all my fans past and present, I hope you enjoy my story.

To everyone at John Blake Publishing, thank you for showing interest in my story and let's hope that we do book number two soon.

Last but not least, I give praise to the Almighty Jehovah God.

CONTENTS

A MOMENT
IN TIME

EVERYONE HAS SEEN her except for me. I can hear the trumpeters playing outside as she steps out of the carriage. All I can do is imagine how she must look, how beautiful her dress his, how soft her skin must feel. So this is it. The big step every kid talks about when they're growing up – getting married and having children. From this moment on I know my life will never be the same.

It feels as if I've been standing here for hours. When I came into the room it was empty. I stood at the front, wondering how on earth I'd come this far. All my life I've dreamed of this day and now it is finally happening. I can hear people walking into the room. Behind me there are gasps of amazement as people admire my Swarovski suit, shimmering in the light. I can't turn around. I want to but I can't turn around.

Of all the achievements in my life, this has to be the greatest. There was a time when all I cared about were number-one singles, adoring fans and sell-out shows at Wembley. But today I am giving my ultimate performance. The final piece of the jigsaw that's been missing for all these years will be finally slotted into place.

When Katie Price walked into my life, she changed my world. I changed her world too. Who'd have thought I'd meet the woman of my dreams on a reality-TV show set in the jungle? It sounds almost unbelievable, but I tell you, it's most certainly true.

It's as if every trial, trauma and tribulation in my life has been leading to this point. And believe me, there have been many. From racist attacks to psychological disturbances, I've been through a lot. I've hit rock bottom so hard I thought I might never reach the surface again. For a long time in my life I forgot what happiness was. Now I understand every dimension, every depth, of that feeling.

A chord strikes. The gospel choir breaks into song. I turn around and glimpse Harvey walking down the aisle, his ear on his shoulder, smiling right at me. Junior, my newborn, is sitting behind me. Both my sons are at my wedding! The singers hit a crescendo.

I know she's in the room. Every hair on my body is standing on end. Shivers are rocketing down my spine. I can hear her coming closer. Now she's standing next to me. I can almost feel her breath on my shoulder. She smells so beautiful. I turn to look at my future wife. Katie Price, the woman who has changed my life for ever. For the first time ever, I feel content. I feel complete.

CHAPTER ONE

HOME AND AWAY

LIFE FOR PETER James Andrea, as I was in those days, began on 27 February 1973 at Northwick Park Hospital in Harrow, north-west London. I was the last child of five boys and a girl. I may have been an accident because I know that after Mum and Dad had had two boys they really wanted a girl. But they just kept getting more boys until they finally had my sister and they were content. Then along I came.

Once I was born, that was the completion of the Andreas. There's 16 years between me and my eldest brother, Andrew. He's 49, Chris is 43, Danny's 38, Michael's 36, Debbie's 35 and I'm the baby at 33. My dad, Savva, was one of 12 kids in Cyprus and wanted a big family himself. Children have always been important for Dad as he's a real family man. Mum, Thea, is the most loving mother. Of course, every kid is going to say that about his mum. But it's true.

When Dad first came to England from Cyprus he was 20.

He'd come to learn a trade, although he didn't speak any English at first. He met Mum in 1954 and they married a year later. For a long time they were really poor, but by the time I arrived they were starting to do well. Dad was a barber and bought a shop at 101 Praed Street in Paddington, right opposite St Mary's Hospital. The shop's still there and Dad still owns it. Mum had her own shop three doors down, where she worked as a seamstress.

There was a lot of love on that street. I used to go down there on Saturdays with Dad in his big Mercedes but I was only allowed to go to his and Mum's shops and sometimes around the corner to Ted's sandwich bar. It was a great treat when Dad would tell me to go to Ted's and get him a ham sandwich, mainly because Ted's wife would always make me a special sandwich for free.

Dad was doing really well. He also owned a women's hair salon underneath his shop and let out rooms above it. And he had houses in Barons Court and Notting Hill too. Back then everything was done in cash and my parents had so much they didn't know where to put it! But I wasn't born with a silver spoon in my mouth. Dad would always tell me, 'Don't think just because you're making money that you will always make money. You've got to work hard.'

Both Dad and Mum insisted their children must earn the good things in life, not expect them as a right. That's still how I think today and before splashing out on a reward like my latest car – a Porsche 911 Carrera – I've always made damn sure I put in some hard work to pay for it.

I remember clearly our house at 1 Sudbury Court Road in Harrow. It was always full of life. We had furry paisley wallpaper and thick green carpets. There was one room we never used, but it was always done up nicely. They call it a *sala* in Greek. No one was allowed in there with their shoes on. We had a 100-foot garden that seemed to go on for ever, with four apple trees at the end. I can recall most of my neighbours and all of my school mates. Of course, there were tough times, but we had some great fun as well.

Because I grew up with brothers and sisters all around me, I had a lot of love. Chris and Debbie each had their own bedroom. Michael, Danny and I had to sleep in one room and sometimes we shared it with Andrew too. I guess that's why we're all so close still. But I never wanted to smell their feet again after that.

Every dinner time we would all sit together at the dining-room table. No one would ever sit in the lounge and watch TV. In our family, meal times were a serious business. After Mum had served up the food, Dad would always say a prayer before we were even allowed to pick up our knives and forks. I remember Chris would kick my leg to try to make me laugh. Because Dad's prayer was always in Greek, we couldn't understand half of what he was saying anyway. But it was always the same routine. We knew exactly the noises he would make at each point and the places where he'd take a breath. We were cheeky little kids and just couldn't wait to eat. The prayer would only last two minutes, but that would sometimes feel like for ever. I remember thinking, Well, he's only got three more breaths to go.

All my brothers were older than me, so they were always served before I was. You couldn't argue with them because they were big boys. One evening when I was about six, I decided to play a trick on Chris. Right, I thought, I'll fix you up! We were having ice cream for dessert and he thought he had one over on me, because Mum had given him a bigger portion than anyone else. I snuck into the kitchen when no one was looking, took a big tablespoon of English mustard and put it right in the middle of his ice cream. Using another spoon, I deftly covered the bright-yellow pile. Chris used to eat so fast he would never dream of looking at exactly what he was putting in his mouth.

I remember the look on poor Chris's face when he took a spoonful – hot mustard mixed with cold ice cream! He threw up so much. My other brothers and sister were rolling around on the floor laughing. But Dad was furious and chased me all over the house. I was scared of him for about a week after that. All these years later we still laugh about it, and every time I offer Chris an ice cream he politely declines and says he'll fetch one himself.

Ours was a very strict household because my parents are Jehovah's Witnesses (devout Christians) and they live their life by the Bible. The key rules were: respect for your elders, clean living and no adultery. These were really a great guide for an upbringing. We'd go to Watchtower classes on Sundays, book study on Tuesdays and Theocratic Ministry meetings on Thursdays. People would be picked to give talks and whenever I was chosen I always thought of myself as a good speaker.

There were no birthday parties or Christmas celebrations, because these are regarded as pagan festivals. I spent my first proper Christmas with Kate two years ago – at the age of 31. But I don't feel as if I missed out on my childhood, because the religion taught me so much. It kept me away from drugs and that's a lifesaver. It also helped me learn manners and the importance of a strong bond with family. I was brought up to understand the reasons behind something, as opposed to just not being allowed to do it, so for me religious rules were never a problem. In fact, to this day I praise the Witnesses.

Most other children at school celebrated Christmas, but I never felt jealous. As strict as my parents were, they were also very fair. While they didn't give us expensive presents, they never let us go without. Mum and Dad always taught us that you don't have to wait until a special occasion to give someone a gift. To this day I still follow the same principle.

Christmas was only ever a hard time for us when we were living in England, and that was because it was always cold and snowing outside. When you don't expect something, you don't get disappointed. When kids at school boasted about the gifts they'd been given, I used to think about everything we had as a family. I always used to try to see the positive side of things and I think that's a trait I inherited from my dad.

A lot of the kids I knew grew up lacking any sense of direction. They may have been outside playing while I was at meetings, but it never bothered me. We were no better or worse than anyone else, but the one thing I can say is that I felt complete.

While I was at Sudbury Junior School my brothers went to Wembley High. They were good schools, although both had their rough elements. Michael, Debbie and I used to go home well protected because one of the teachers, a wonderful lady called Mrs Bye, lived in our road. When I was first at school she would walk us home because our parents kept a very tight hold on us. But when I got to six I was allowed to walk home without her. That was when I met my first girlfriend, Miranda Madurasinghe, a Sri Lankan. It was the real thing all right. We used to hold hands under the desk and at six years old that feels like the most amazing thing. I remember INXS brought out a song called 'Original Sin' which referred to the dream of love between a white boy and a black girl. That was how it was with Miranda and I. We were in love. Remember when you kiss for the first time and it's just lips and a closed mouth? It seems to last for ever. After I moved away we continued to write to each other for years. Miranda lived in Wood End Road in Sudbury and the first time I came back to England, in 1992, to record some tracks, I was so determined to see her that I went to her house and found she was still living there. We hit it off straight away, but it wasn't the same feeling. I'll never forget her mum, she was so lovely to me.

My school reports weren't great. OK, they were bad. I was in trouble all the time because I was the kid who never started a fight but was always in the middle of one. I always wanted to protect the underdog. I guess that's part of being a show-off as a kid – you want be the hero. If I saw two boys beating up another one I'd always have to wade in to rescue him. Then I'd get the guys that were bothering him turning on me. Even the boy I'd saved would be so scared that he'd side with them and they'd all start on me. That's how it happened every time. Eventually the headmaster, Mr Harris, sent me to a psychologist after failing with both the cane

and what we called the 'plimsoll pudding'. Corporal
punishment was still legal then.

At home I was always very scared of Dad, although it was
my three elder brothers who got the worst of it, as he
disciplined them quite hard. They would often get a wallop,
but that was no different from many other families. What I
was really scared of was Dad's voice, which used to make me
shake. Even when the two of us talk now, there's still a sense
of fear when I hear certain tones. Whenever it was school-
report time I'd run up to my room when Dad came home, as
I was never a high achiever. I'd pray to God that Mum had
received my report because she couldn't understand
English. Before Dad had seen it I'd explain it to her and lie a
bit. Always a mummy's boy, I'd run to her because I knew
she'd tone everything down when she told Dad about me.

I would never answer back to my dad. To this day I've
never said the words 'shut up' or even 'shhh' to him. Nor
have I ever sworn at either of my parents. All my brothers
smoke but, out of respect for Mum and Dad, not one of them
ever does so in front of them. That's why I find Kate's family
so bizarre. She swears at her mum and talks about sex. That
doesn't mean her way is wrong and mine is right; it's just
that they are completely different. But, if one of our kids
turns around and swears at me, I will not be lenient. They'll
be grounded. It's really important to me that they have
respect for their parents and older people in general.

During my childhood Mum was pure love. I don't
remember Dad picking me up and holding me. There was no
'I love you', no hugs – nothing like that. Not that he didn't
love me. I know he did, but his strict way of life meant he

couldn't bring himself to say it. But I'm so close to him now. Just a few weeks ago he said to me, 'I'm sorry I didn't hold you. Maybe I should have done.' Wow, I thought, I'm 33 and I'm hearing that from my dad, who's in his seventies! As I've grown up Dad has become a great friend. I've always wanted to make him proud, but over time that changes from a fear that you'll be punished to a fear that you'll break their heart. For instance, I remember going to a Carlsberg festival with Dad when I was 12. We stopped at traffic lights and suddenly a guy on a motorcycle crashed into a car in front. It was the most horrific thing I've ever seen.

Dad turned to me and clearly said, 'All I want you to do is promise me you'll never ride a motorbike.'

To this day I've kept that promise. While my father is alive I will never ride a motorbike; that's the kind of respect I have for him.

It wasn't just Dad I was scared of as a kid. The world outside was becoming a dangerous place, with something bad always going on. I remember my brother Chris came in with blood on his hands after he'd got in a fight and someone had stabbed him. Later I found out it was his so-called best friend who had done it.

One day in our friendly little street, two gangs on motorbikes roared up and started fighting with chains. One guy ended up crashing through the window of a passing car. My world was changing and I was petrified. Ours was no longer the cool little street where all the neighbours were friendly. Now everyone was locking their doors and nervously peering out from behind the curtains. There was a fear on our street. I even used to go upstairs at night and look under the beds and in the cupboards in case a bad man was hiding there.

That was when Mum and Dad started talking about moving to Australia. They wanted to bring us up in safety, and being near the sea and in the sunshine would be an added bonus. At first it all sounded like a dream to me, but as the big day of our departure in 1979 drew near I couldn't bear the idea of being separated from my friends, especially my six-year-old girlfriend Miranda, my good mate Jamie Roberts and my teacher Mrs Bye. I had such mixed feelings: excitement and happiness about a huge adventure and a new way of life, but tears about leaving so much behind that was dear to me, and fears about what lay ahead. To me, Australia was the great unknown.

There had been no great family conference to decide if emigrating was what we all wanted. Mum and Dad didn't do things that way. They just sat us down at the table one day and said, 'Get packed because we're going to be moving to Australia.' To begin with, we thought of it as a holiday, but later the truth slowly sank in. We were about to move to the other side of the world and it was hard to take in. Mum cried a lot; I don't think she wanted to go. I know Dad did, though, because, while half of his brothers and sisters had moved to Britain, the others had all settled in Australia.

I was just worried about music, which back then I already loved with a passion – especially Motown. That's what my brothers would bring home – Luther Vandross, James Ingram, Al Green. So I ran upstairs and recorded ten of my favourite songs from the radio, mainly soul and reggae numbers. I couldn't live without them while I was in Oz.

But surely, I thought, they must play music like that Down Under?

That music would be my last memory of England, I thought. I didn't know if I'd ever come back. So I took that cassette with me and listened to it on the plane over and over and over again. Little did I know that this would be the last time I really felt at home until 26 years later, when I met Kate.

CHAPTER TWO

FINDING MY VOICE

AFTER A FLIGHT that seemed to go on for ever, we touched down in Sydney. A new life began. Sun, sand, surf – every cliché you hear about Australia really is true. We met up with long-lost relatives, aunts, uncles and cousins I had never seen, and soon we all felt at home.

Life in Sydney seemed so natural. Then one day my parents went for a holiday on the Gold Coast in Queensland with my uncle Jack, who knew the place well, and fell in love with it. Dad got itchy feet again and decided we should move up there instead. As it happens, it was in Queensland, 20-something years later, that I went into the jungle for *I'm A Celebrity Get Me Out Of Here* and my whole life was turned upside down – again.

As a kid, I couldn't understand why we'd moved all the way to Sydney so that Dad could be with all his brothers and sisters and now he wanted to move a thousand kilometres away to Queensland. I was really confused. Mum and Dad had moved to Australia in search of a better life and it certainly was the land of opportunity. At six years old, though, I couldn't have known how living there would shape me in the way it did and change the whole course of my life.

The Gold Coast was great, very natural and under-developed. They have a saying in Queensland, 'Beautiful one day, perfect the next', and they're not wrong. There were no high-rise blocks, no noisy traffic jams – just beautiful crystal-white beaches as far as the eye could see. I was like a kid in a candy store.

Our new home town was heaven for surfers; it's even called Surfers Paradise. The beach, just minutes from our house, was beautiful and, unlike the way it is today, was completely unspoiled by development. It's still beautiful, just different. We were never allowed to go there alone, however, because now we faced a new danger. Not other people's violence, as in London, but the sharks, bluebottle jellyfish, box jellyfish and a thousand other nasties in the sea that could give you a serious, possibly fatal, bite or sting. We even had to learn to swim in a pool above Paradise Towers, the building where Mum and Dad each ran their own business.

But in fact the worst threat to us kids was on dry land. My parents and my brothers drummed into Debbie and me that Aussie spiders could harm us, and quite naturally we were mighty scared. Once you've seen two or three of these massive things walking around your house you start to develop a bit of a phobia.

The people in Queensland were also very different from what we had been used to. They weren't accustomed to

Greeks and Italians, and they used to call us wogs, which in the part of London where I grew up was a derogatory term used against black people.

In England I'd never been teased about the way I looked, but it was a different story in Australia. It began within three days of my starting school. I was Greek, with dark hair and dark eyes, but all the other kids were blonde with blue eyes. Talk about being the odd one out! Aussie kids would tie me to a fence, throw stones at me and beat me up. It was horrible and very soon I associated school with fights. Even the teachers picked on me because I had an English accent. There was so much racism and I realised I was the complete underdog because I was ethnically different. Even though I'd get the shit beaten out of me by other kids, I was always too proud to cry.

The bullying made me feel like such an outcast, which was a totally new experience for me – and one I didn't like at all. When you are the victim of bullying at school, it makes you dread having to go in and face another day. I felt so isolated and distant from the other kids; even if we were all sat around the same table, say at lunch, I felt like I may as well have been sitting a million miles away from them. For years, my school days were gut-wrenchingly miserable.

You might ask why I didn't go to my parents, my brothers or my teachers to tell them what was going on. It was simple – no one likes a grass. I was disliked enough as it was, so I was hardly about to make myself even more unpopular by being denounced for being a snitch on top of everything else. Despite my best efforts, my brothers still sometimes got wind of the fact that I was being picked on and would step in to 'sort out' my tormentors. While it was very nice of them to help me out, more often than not, the bullies' older brothers would retaliate and the whole thing would escalate into a huge fight of war-like proportions.

Eventually, I could no longer bear to have these low-lifes making my life so miserable and at 13 years old took matters into my own hands. Against my dad's wishes, I took up martial arts. Eventually, I became proficient in several disciplines including Muay Thai (kick boxing), Wing Chun Kung Fu and Chow Gar Tong Long (another kind of Kung Fu, in which the stance of the Preying Mantis is adopted). I also did boxing for a few years. The great thing about these martial arts is that the emphasis is not on aggression, but on self-defence. And once the bullies became aware that I had the power to defend myself, the abuse gradually stopped. Not by instigating violence, but by having the confidence and the skill to know I could stand up to my aggressors physically, I was able to get my life back on track.

Fortunately, I've never had to use my martial arts skills and I never want to; but at least I know I can protect my family if I need to. I think it would be good for Junior to learn self-defence, which, as well as teaching him to defend himself, will also teach discipline. He and Harvey will eventually get picked on a lot at school and I want Junior to be there for his older brother, although I'd never allow him to start a fight.

One day Dad was driving me to school and I heard a song on the radio that stuck in my mind. That song, 'Wherever I Lay My Hat, That's My Home' by Paul Young, used to make me very sad, because, although Australia was now my

14

home, I started missing what I'd had in England. I felt lost and I didn't like it one little bit.

After school I would go home and listen religiously, over and over again, to the tape I'd put together in London. I refused to tune into Australian radio stations, I refused to watch Australian video clips. My musical life was that ten-track tape. At night I would go up to my room, where I had pictures on the wall of Elvis, Stevie Wonder, Michael Jackson and Bob Marley, and suddenly I'd be transported to a world of magic. I'd look at Elvis, close my eyes, imagine I was him and sing one of his songs, mimicking his voice as best I could.

Singing had always been an important part of my life, but when I was young most of the singing I did was at Jehovah's Witnesses' meetings in Wembley. I was always singing, but I didn't know that my heart's desire was to sing for a living until I went to Australia. Then I couldn't do without it. I was constantly practising; practising for what, I had no idea. I just needed it. It took me to a place where I wanted to be.

The very first album I bought in Australia was a vinyl copy of Michael Jackson's *Off the Wall*. This was my getaway, my freedom. I'd go upstairs, put the album on and think back to England and all the friends I was missing. That was all I had, because at first I had no friends in Australia.

And that's when I started developing what I called my 'pop dream'. I set myself a goal of going back to England one day and appearing on *Top of the Pops*.

I remember reading about how Michael Jackson would be rehearsing while his friends were out playing ball and he would stare out of the window and wonder, Why am I not like them? Of course, it was all for a bigger purpose. I used to do the same. I used to look out of the window and think, Why aren't I like those kids in the park? I always felt like an outsider – always.

Every day I'd rush home from school and whip through my homework in ten or fifteen minutes. Needless to say, I didn't make a very good job of it. Once I'd conned Dad into believing I'd finished all my work properly, I'd go up to my room, stand in front of the pictures of my favourite artists and practise singing just like them – over and over again. I used to sing until my throat was so sore I just had to stop. What drove me on was my dream that one day I would be accepted by all those people who treated me as an outsider. I knew I couldn't change the colour of my skin, or the way I look, but I was sure I could be their equal if I could make it as a singer.

The only person who really believed in me at that time was my brother Chris. He was a musician and he knew that I had something. I wasn't the greatest singer but I had a confidence about me. I wanted so much to become great. Dancing was also important to me. I hated to look at a singer on stage and think they were boring. I always wanted them to be moving.

Before long I'd left my bedroom and made the garage my live stage. I got Dad to buy me these great speakers and I agreed to pay him back a dollar a week – which he never took from me, of course! I would always pretend to be on stage, and at last I had the opportunity to sing in public at the school show when I was 13. It was all a very last-minute thing. The lead singer couldn't do it and my music teacher,

Mrs Challenger, gave me a chance. I loved Stevie Wonder, so I sang 'I Just Called To Say I Love You'. I was petrified yet at the same time confident as I performed before an audience of a thousand people. Their response was incredibly positive.

'You've got something,' my music teacher turned to me and said. 'You can do it.'

When you get that sort of encouragement it boosts you.

Life was starting to get better. I'd already started a new school, Benowa High – Benowa is Aborigine for 'clear water' – and I was beginning to make some friends. George Nicolau, from Canberra, was also a Greek-Cypriot and we faced a lot of the torment of racist taunts and bullying together. Little did I suspect that one day he would be best man at my wedding. What made George such a really true friend was that he always felt that whatever happened to me should also happen to him. We had so much fun together too; we even dated twin sisters once, which was quite handy to say the least!

Over time I became part of a tight-knit group of friends. We created our own little Rat Pack and very soon we were the ones getting all the attention. The Rat Pack were the most popular kids at school. Much of our popularity was down to Christian Fry. He was the good-looking kid at Benowa High and the girls were crazy about him. Then there was Cardiff Smith, a tall redhead, Craig Ball, an aspiring actor, and me. I was now known at school as Peter Andre. The final 'a' had been dropped a few years earlier when my brother Mike started school. Kids didn't realise that it wasn't pronounced, so he would shout at them, 'It's not Andrea, it's Andre, you idiot.' They started calling him Michael Andre, so when I started coming to the school I was obviously Peter Andre. And that's how it happened. Christian and I both started practising martial arts, which proved to be a real hit with the girls. As soon as I learned how to defend myself, I was actually involved in fewer fights. People backed off. Mike, who was two years above me, was also a good fighter and had formed his own respected clique. That little bit of power gave me popularity and before I knew it everything had changed.

It was around this time that I started working out at the gym. We had a police–citizens youth club near where we lived and Michael, Danny and sometimes Chris would go down to the gym there and lift weights. In the room next door was a punchbag that you could box or kick-box, and that was where I would go while my brothers built up their bodies. Incredibly skinny, I couldn't lift even the lightest weights, and because I was so young my brothers made sure I didn't do anything that would hurt me.

So three or four times a week I'd hit the bag until I was puffed out – which was usually after about five minutes. Then I'd drop down on the mat and do sit-ups for an hour and a half. I used to ask my brothers, 'Do you think by the time I'm 16 I'll have abs?'

Everyone used to say, 'Well, if you keep doing that you will.' Sure enough, just after my fifteenth birthday I started to notice these ripples of muscle down my stomach. I was still as skinny as a rake, but I had abs to die for. Trouble was, once I got them they became an obsession. Soon training took over my life. At school all I could think about was the lunch break when I could nip into the gym to work out.

My sister Debbie put herself on a low-fat diet and I became

devoted to watching what she ate. I stopped eating the chips and lamb chops that Mum would make at night and before I knew it I had more energy and I didn't feel sluggish. Every morning I'd make a drink with raw eggs, banana, honey and protein powder. I was a full-on health freak. Mornings I used to go running on the beach in thick sand so that it would be like running in the snow.

My body became something I was immensely proud of – to the point of vanity. But it's like the rich man who's never happy with his riches – he wants more. I was never happy with my body. I always wanted more, more, more.

I watched movies like *Kick Boxer*, starring Jean-Claude Van Damme, and *Enter the Dragon* with Bruce Lee. Guys want to be like them and girls want to be with them. One day I'm gonna be a singer version of these guys, I told myself. In my heart I knew I could be somebody. I never thought I could be as big as I was when finally I did make it. It was never about the money – I just wanted recognition. I wanted to be as popular at school as all the other boys. I did it almost to become normal, rather than to become better than the rest.

As my body improved, so did my luck with girls. My first sexual encounter took place when I was 14. There was word around school that a certain girl liked giving oral pleasure to guys. I desperately wanted to be like all the other guys, so I asked her if she'd do it with me. I went to see her with my friend Peter and we arranged to meet her after school. Because of my religious beliefs I did feel guilty about what we did, but also there was suddenly a sense of 'Yes, I'm like everyone else'.

Our Rat Pack was wild – girls, partying, drinking,

nightclubs on Thursday night, Friday night, Saturday night, even Sunday night. I felt it was time to make up for all those years when I'd been picked on and laughed at. At last I'd been accepted and I wanted to let myself loose. I just wanted to behave like every other 16-year-old. My brothers had friends on the nightclub circuit, so I always found it easy to get past the bouncers. The big drinks for young teenagers were Southern Comfort and Coke or beer. Later on I got into Sambuca, vodka and all that stronger stuff.

I knew I was being hypocritical about my beliefs because I enjoyed the time with my mates so much. Deep inside I wanted to stop going to the Sunday meetings of the Jehovah's Witnesses, even though I still loved what I learned there. I'd reached the age, like most teenagers, where I felt I wanted to be at home practising my music or hanging out with my friends, not worshipping God. I could see I was attending the Witness meetings to please Mum and Dad, which was the wrong reason.

I knew I was now into a totally different way of life. Yet I never felt guilty for being drunk, even though my religion's rules were to drink 'in moderation'. As far as I was concerned, I was moderately having fun! I simply adapted the religious teachings to work for me. Basically, I was kidding myself. According to the Witnesses, God detests somebody sitting on the fence. One thing I've never wanted to be is a hypocrite. Suddenly, I began asking myself, Why are you still going to the Witness meetings and pretending to be a good boy, when in fact you're breaking every rule? So I started to skip the meetings. However, to this day, I love what I learned and will always respect the Witnesses.

I would never drink in front of Mum and Dad, as I hate being out of control around the people I love. My biggest source of guilt was that I'd disappoint my parents. I knew I wasn't going to change and I knew that I wanted to drink, go to clubs and be with girls. The only thing I had left was respect for my parents, so I kept misbehaving but always away from home. I'm sure Mum and Dad knew what was going on, and it was a hard part of my life, because for the first time I felt unable to communicate with them.

I waited until I was 17 to have full intercourse – that's how long the guilt stayed with me. Melanie Cooper was in the year below me and we were in the same drama class. She was different from all the other girls I'd been with, because I really did like her. Funnily enough, she's probably the only blonde girl I've ever been with apart from Kate. We became really good friends and eventually an item. Every time we kissed and touched it was so much more special than with anyone else. But I was always scared to take that final step. Then, out of the blue, it happened.

It was a really hot night on the Gold Coast. We were in her apartment and the windows were wide open and we could hear the sea. Our favourite Anita Baker album was playing and she leaned over to light up some candles. We were kissing and touching and one thing led to another. I felt this overwhelming sense of inevitability. It was incredible, but afterwards I felt so ashamed that I'd betrayed my beliefs; that I'd really gone too far this time. That sense of guilt has always been with me, right up until the minute Kate and I married. With Kate I have a wild sex life, but for the first time it feels normal.

I stayed with Melanie for about a year and a half. Once you've shared an experience like that with someone, you don't want to lose them. Now they own a part of you and you want to stay together. But then I messed it all up. Melanie moved with her family to New Zealand, but as far as our relationship was concerned she might just as well have gone to the moon. I missed her and I wanted her to come back, but after a couple of months I convinced myself I was never going to see her again and I started dating someone else.

Then one night Melanie suddenly turned up again without telling me she was back on the Gold Coast. She wanted it to be a surprise. And boy, was it! I was with another girl and Melanie was devastated. I broke her heart and she didn't want to know me. I felt terrible. My first adult relationship had ended disastrously. Unfortunately, I didn't learn from my mistakes. As I became increasingly selfish and self-obsessed, screwing up relationships would become a familiar story.

CHAPTER THREE
POP DREAM ...
POP NIGHTMARE

IT WASN'T JUST my interest in girls that was growing stronger. I was now more determined than ever to make my pop dream come true. I started to enter local talent competitions in pubs and bars, where week after week I'd get up and sing 'Stand By Me' by Ben E. King, 'My Girl' by the Temptations or 'Ain't No Sunshine' by Bill Withers. My brother Chris used to make the backing tracks for me and I'd sing the vocal live. There was no way you could mime – you had to sing well or you were out on your arse. The other members of the Rat Pack, Christian, Cardiff and Craig, always supported me and they felt my failures as deeply as I did. But I kept plugging away.

Then one day I watched a talent show on TV called *New Faces* and I knew I had to get on it. Everyone kept urging me to audition but I was too frightened. I wasn't ready, although I knew my time would come. Unfortunately, the show was dropped and I'd left it too late. By this time I was desperate, so I started phoning Channel 9 TV in Sydney. Every Monday morning I'd manage to be off school 'sick' and every Monday at 9am the same woman would pick up the phone at Channel 9 and get me on the line. Her name was Shauna Kane and she was such a sweet lady. No matter how much I pestered her, she always stayed calm, and talking to her helped give me the confidence I needed. Our Monday-morning conversations were always the same.

'Please can I audition for the show?'

'I'm sorry – the show's off the air.'

'Please, please – I really want to do it, I really want to do it.'

'Sorry, that's impossible. But I like your determination.'

I kept ringing for month after month and singing down the phone to my audience of one. When the phone bills came in I'd get screamed at by Dad, who'd worked out what was going on.

'You're wasting your time and my money,' he'd yell – in a loving way, of course!

And I kept wasting it for another nine months, until one Monday morning I made my usual call to Shauna and was told: 'Peter – you're not gonna believe this.'

'What?'

'The show's going back on air and guess where the first place we're auditioning is. Queensland.'

At first Dad was against me entering, but eventually, when he realised how much this opportunity meant to me, he let me go. I travelled with Danny to another audition in Melbourne, where I planned to sing the Bobby Brown number 'Every Little Step'. Halfway through my performance I noticed Shauna was crying and I thought I'd messed up. In fact, she was simply so pleased that my dream was finally coming true. To my amazement, she said the words I'd waited almost a year to hear: 'You're in.'

One of the *New Faces* judges was a man called Ian 'Molly' Meldrum, who was the Simon Cowell or Pete Waterman of Australia. Molly could make – or break, as I learned later – a career. He had been a rock journalist who worked for the Beatles at London's Abbey Road Studios in the 1960s. When the Beatles did a concert at Melbourne's Festival Hall, Molly was thrown out of the audience for getting overexcited! Luckily, he wasn't one of the judges at my audition, but when I appeared on the show two weeks later he was there on the panel.

The host was Darryl Summers, Australia's Saturday-night king, who had a massive Channel 9 show called *Hey Hey It's Saturday*. Just the thought of appearing in front of those two huge showbiz names, never mind the studio audience and a million or two who'd be watching from home when the show went out the following Saturday, gave me the shakes.

When the night of my TV performance eventually came, I was shitting myself with nerves. There were seven acts in Studio 9: me, three other vocalists, a juggler, a comedian and a dancer. Was I confident? Not on your life. I knew I could sing, and after hours of trying this and trying that I'd changed my mind and gone for Bobby Brown's 'Don't Be Cruel'. I knew I could dance and one of Danny's friends, Victor, had helped me choreograph all the moves. The only thing that worried me was whether I could put it all together on what was the biggest night so far of my 16 years.

As I stood there, my face as white as a sheet (which isn't easy for a Greek guy, believe me!), I told myself, 'Please don't be last. Just don't be last.' Years later I would say the same thing to myself as I prayed I wouldn't be the first to be voted out of the jungle. There was no way I could fail and face an already hostile crowd of kids at school. I was the last to perform and, to make matters worse, the guy before me scored an all-time record number of points.

'I can't do it – I've got to go home,' I blabbed to Danny like a big girl.

'Yeah,' he said, nearly in tears himself. 'All right, you go. But just think of that huge amount of effort wasted.'

Then Victor gave me a Mars bar and said, 'Don't be daft, mate. This is your big chance, you can't blow it now. Eat this chocolate to give yourself some energy and then get up there and do it.'

So there I was, seconds from going live in front of the cameras, in a black and white polka-dot waistcoat I'd borrowed from my brother Michael and with what now seems a ridiculous hairstyle – short back 'n' sides, flat top, but some long hair at the back tied back in a little ponytail. It was really – ugh! And I had black trousers, black shoes and – wait for it – *white* socks. Jackson or what? I look back on it now and I can't stop laughing. That night I was close to crying. But I stayed focused and, when the floor manager waved his arm to tell me I was on air, I took a deep breath to calm my nerves, stepped out in front of the cameras and gave it my best shot.

The live band started up and all I could do was think of my vocal pitching and my looks to camera. I really went for it, but was I nervous! I went through what thousands go through today on *The X Factor* and *Pop Idol*. It's so daunting and not an experience I'd want to repeat.

Then, to my horror, Darryl announced we were going to a commercial break before the judges could deliver their verdict. So, as I faced an agonising three minutes' wait, I was petrified, sure I was going to get a slating. But when the crucial moment came I couldn't believe what I was hearing.

'You are a natural,' said the first judge. 'You're a star.'

The audience went wild and my heart was pounding so hard it seemed I could hear it.

The second judge was a choreographer, so I had high hopes that he would have appreciated my routine.

'I'd like to have seen slightly more versatility in your moves,' he said, 'but, as for star quality, you've definitely got it.'

He was right. I had taken every Jackson move I knew and caned it!

Boy, how could anyone top that? I thought.

Then, last but by no means least, it was Molly Meldrum's turn. He just came straight out with it: 'I wouldn't mind you coming to talk with me. I own Melodian Records and I think you're it! You're going to be a huge star.'

Those words were what I had dreamed about, what I had worked so hard for and waited so long to hear. All I could think of was getting out of the studio as fast as possible so that I could ring home and tell Mum and Dad their little boy had won. All the contestants had been warned to keep the results a secret, but I was bursting to share the news.

That night the TV people put me up in a beautiful hotel, the first time in my life I'd experienced such luxury, with champagne and chocolates in my room. I was buzzing now, but I knew that for five days I was not allowed to tell anyone. No one in history had been signed up live on air on *New Faces*.

Three months had passed since the *New Faces* final and I couldn't understand why I hadn't heard a word from Molly Meldrum about the record deal. I said to Mum and Dad, 'Maybe it's not going to happen, maybe it's all just been a dream.' I started to become depressed – something that was to return and haunt me later in my career. I couldn't face going to school, where people would pester me with, 'Have you heard?' and I'd have to tell them, 'No, not yet.'

Another three months went by and I wasn't sure how much longer I could take the waiting and the wondering. Then one brilliant day a director from Mushroom Records called Simon contacted me and said he was flying up to Surfers Paradise. Wow! It was what I'd been waiting to hear. Molly's Melodian label was a branch of Mushroom. Dad had already told me, 'If you don't get anywhere with your music by the time you've finished school, you're going to college.' That was a lot of pressure for me to cope with. Luckily my parents now said I could sign the contract with Mushroom on the last day of term.

Of course, at just 16 I didn't know anything about contracts and the law. I was so naive I couldn't even sniff out a good deal or a bad deal when it was right under my nose. And, boy, oh boy, this was not the best deal – even though, according to them, I was potentially one of the best acts on Mushroom's books!

Why it took two years from my success on *New Faces* to release a single, I'll never know. Mushroom said they wanted to 'nurture' my career. 'Drive Me Crazy' struggled to reach number 72 and they decided 'Gimme Little Sign' would be my ticket to stardom. I absolutely hated it. To me it was so cheesy. And cheesy was to haunt me for years.

Worse was to come. Despite his name, I didn't know that Molly was gay and famous for signing young boy bands, especially 'good-looking' ones, apparently. Throughout the industry, and especially in the music press, the whispers were going round that I must be gay too. They thought I was Molly's toyboy. Nothing could have been further from the truth. I may have had a pretty face, but I was only interested in girls. I don't have a problem with anyone's sexual preferences, but being accused of something you are not is wrong.

Things reached a head a few years later when an art magazine called *Black and White* asked me to pose naked. That was a definite problem for me. I was still only 19 then and not as open-minded as I am today. When I was young, posing naked in a magazine could mean only one thing. I protested strongly, but Molly had other ideas. I had no choice.

The shots were arty and nothing rude was on show, but I hated every minute of the shoot. When the magazine eventually came out, my parents were devastated and it caused them real embarrassment. Plus, in the back of my mind I knew I was just fuelling all those rumours.

To be honest, Molly never made advances towards me. But I always felt uncomfortable and I started to resent homosexuals because of the tag that was being put on me. It's like being told you're a drug addict when you've never even taken a pill in your whole life. Ironically, today two of my and Kate's best friends, Gary and Phil, are a happily married couple and the clubs I like performing at best are gay clubs. Now I've grown up and I'm completely comfortable with myself and my sexuality I can be more open-minded.

The video for 'Gimme Little Sign' was shot in brilliant sunshine on Bondi Beach and the production company, Perpetual Motion Pictures, made it look a million dollars – just like Elvis's *Blue Hawaii*. There were a couple of great girl dancers, one a beautiful blonde Australian, the other a beautiful dark, Greek-looking girl, and the whole thing oozed sex appeal. Hopefully, it meant people would now be attracted to the image as well as to the song. But that presented me with a new problem. Although the rest of the world knew nothing about it, I'd been dating a dancer called Kathy Maddock for some time now. My record company ordered me to keep quiet about my girlfriend in case it upset any potential fans.

'You mention her and your career's not going to happen,' I was told brutally. So poor Kathy was kept out of the limelight. She went through hell, because she really loved me. And I loved her too – but my priority was my career. Years later I bitterly regretted the way I treated Kathy, because she deserved much better. But at the time I selfishly believed I had made the right decision in pushing her into the background. Thanks in no small part to the video, 'Gimme Little Sign' was massive and went straight in at number three. I was the first solo singer in Australia to be that big and I was featured on the cover of all the magazines. Sadly, the more my fame grew the more I pushed Kathy to one side.

Everyone in the music industry – from agents to journalists to fans – thought I was young, free and single, while the truth was that I was in a deep relationship, though one that was being put under very heavy strain. It was inevitable that one day Kathy and I would split, however hard I tried to keep us together. As my popularity grew I found it harder to remain faithful. Cheating on my girlfriend is not something I'm proud of, but back then I was young and selfish.

One day I was sitting downstairs at Mushroom Records when a phone call came from the big boss, Michael Gudinski, who promoted artists such as Madonna, and Sir Elton John in Australia. He also managed the late Michael Hutchence. 'Is Peter Andre in the building?' he asked the receptionist. 'Send him upstairs.'

I was messing myself on the way up to his palatial office. I thought he was going to chew me off for using the company phones or something, but I was in for a shock. Michael was as nice as pie.

'You've been working very hard,' he said. 'You're doing very well. How'd you like to open up for Bobby Brown on his tour?'

'B... B... Bobby B... B... Brown?' I said. 'Are you kidding? Of course I'll do it.'

What a dream! Two years earlier I'd used Bobby's song to win *New Faces* and now I was going to open the show for him all round Australia. The first time I met Bobby at rehearsals I was awestruck. It was all I could do to speak. This man was an idol to me.

'Waddup, Dawg?' he said.

'Hey, BB, how ya doin'?' was all I could manage to stammer.

He was a superstar but he instantly put me at ease. He was so charming and so grateful to me for doing him the honour, as he put it, of joining him on his tour. Believe me, the privilege was all mine. But I wasn't just doing a warm-up spot before the big man came on. No, I did a 90-minute set with a live band – and none other than my brother Chris on guitar as my very own, and very special, support act.

Bobby and I toured the length and breadth of Australia and we became pretty good mates, or so I naively thought. What I didn't realise at the time was that he liked to get close to the young girls who were hanging around the shows. Bobby is married to Whitney Houston. Bizarrely, he even wrote a song called '(Ain't Nobody) Humpin' Around'.

It was on that tour that I first saw people taking class A drugs, particularly cocaine. My strict upbringing paid off, because I always managed to resist the temptation.

At the time, I was seeing a girl, who I'll call Aisha, behind Kathy's back. A stunner with dark skin and green eyes, Aisha was on tour with me. People from Bobby's band kept ringing my hotel room, inviting me to parties after each show, and I thought it was because they enjoyed my company. In fact, one of them had his eye on Aisha.

One night, Aisha and I were in a club with the guys and I was hating it. Cocaine was being shared around by some of the crowd as if it was candy and it slowly dawned on me that Aisha and this one particular guy were developing the hots for each other. But I was too naive to realise they would end up in bed together that night. When it was time to go, Aisha wouldn't come back to the hotel with me. It was ten o'clock the next morning before she showed up. I wonder what on earth she could have possibly been up to ...

Just 18 when I was on that tour, I was away from home for more than a few days for the first time. It was a big, scary world out there. I suffered dehydration and couldn't eat because I was so nervous. But that was the least of my problems. Molly started giving me hell and putting me down at every opportunity, but I felt that if I wanted my career to continue I had to pretend to be his friend.

I co-wrote enough good material for an album called, with great originality, *Peter Andre*, and I was really proud of it. Over a period of time it went gold in Australia, a huge achievement for a solo artist. By then I had built up a huge fan base and the person who mattered most had started to take notice of me again. I got my second call to go up to Michael Gudinski's office.

'Hey, Andre,' he said, as if he'd forgotten my first name. 'You did really well on the Bobby tour. You did really well with the album. How would you like to open for Madonna?'

Wow! A six-week tour – not in small arenas like I had been

doing with Bobby Brown, but in stadiums. I'd be opening for Madonna on her Girlie tour. For days I couldn't contain my excitement at the prospect of performing in front of that crowd. When I met Madonna backstage in Melbourne she was everything I had imagined her to be – but better. What a confident and sexy lady! And she was very sweet to me, although I know she'd never heard of me before.

I saw her in Los Angeles about a year later when we were both recording at the same studio. 'Hi, how are you?' I said, but she looked blank. So I tried, 'Look, this sounds stupid. I don't know if you remember me but I opened the whole of your Australian tour for you.'

And she just looked me up and down and said, 'No, I don't recall that at all. Am I supposed to?'

That's the music business for you.

Regardless, after performing with Madonna and Bobby Brown I was at the peak of my career. I now had a sizeable fan base and I was preparing to do my own arena tour. Unfortunately, not everyone shared the enthusiasm for my success. Once again racism crept in and I received death threats from several Middle-Eastern gangs. I was getting knives pulled on me at clubs and letters sent to my home address saying things like, 'I hope your mum and dad are going to sleep well tonight because we're keeping a close eye. Tell them not to sleep too deeply.'

One night in King's Cross, Sydney's red-light district, I was surrounded in the street by about a dozen thugs. They circled me really slowly, then suddenly one of them pulled out a knife and that was the signal for the whole gang to produce knives and chains. One guy spat at me, 'My brother's in hospital because of you. If my brother dies, I take your life. We all take your life!'

Was I hearing right? I had absolutely no idea what he was going on about.

'Give me one good reason why I shouldn't slice you up now,' the guy said.

I could think of plenty of good reasons, but he was in no mood to listen. Fortunately for me, that night he and his friends were all talk and no action. But I still shudder when I think what might have happened.

It was a long time before I found out what had prompted that unprovoked attack. One of the gang had a brother whose girlfriend liked my songs and told him, 'I'd do anything to go to a Peter Andre concert.' It was a perfectly innocent remark, but the boyfriend was a jealous guy and got really angry because he thought his girlfriend fancied me more than him. So he hit her across the face. A couple of blokes saw this happen from across the street and ran over and beat the hell out of the guy, putting him into intensive care. And I got the blame for that! I was tormented for so long, not knowing why it was that people seemed to hate me with such a passion. I stored up so much fear and hatred inside that it started eating me up.

The hatred I encountered was not restricted to Sydney, though. Even back on my home turf on the Gold Coast I ran into trouble. There were many different gangs in the area and it seemed certain ones in particular had it in for me. One night, I was in a nightclub called Cocos with my brother Michael. Because of who I was, these guys started a fight with my brother. Security picked me up and shoved

The happiest man alive – with my beautiful wife Katie at Disneyland in Orlando.

Above: This was taken just after we moved to Australia, in 1979. *From left to right*: My brother Danny, me (no six-pack yet!) and my sister Debbie.

Below: Wow, what a mullet! This school photo shows me aged fifteen (*middle row, second from the left*).

Thriller! I loved performing from an early age. This is me aged thirteen when I made it to the final of a Michael Jackson competition in Australia. His music was a real inspiration to me throughout my career.

The early days of my music career – on location at Sydney's Bondi Beach to film the video for 'Gimme Little Sign'. I hated the song at the time, but I was proved wrong as it was a huge hit – so I can't complain.

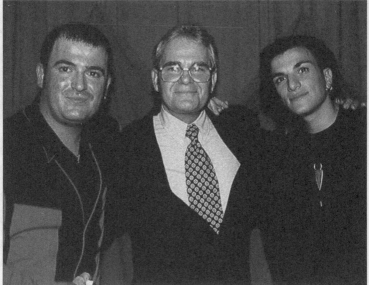

Above: A giant cake to celebrate my 21st birthday.

Below: My brother, Chris, Aussie sports guru Les Murray and myself backstage at the Madonna concert, 1994.

Opening for Madonna on the Australian leg of her Girlie Tour was a great lift-off for my career.

Above: Shooting the 'Mysterious Girl' video in Thailand.

Below left: One of my first big breaks was opening for Bobby Brown on his Australian tour. I was just eighteen then, and the experience certainly opened my eyes!

Below right: Some decorations for the living room wall! With my brothers Mike and Chris, receiving awards from Australia and New Zealand in 1996.

Above left: Backstage at one of my sell-out gigs with former England midfielder, Steve McManaman, 1997.

Above right: With Halle Berry at the Word Music Awards in Monaco, 1998.

Below: Proudly holding my World Music Award for Best Australian Artist.

me into a back room and soon enough the gang – and the trouble – disappeared. We were then told to leave because our presence there was causing too much of a problem.

Only later did I learn that, after we had left, these guys had returned to the nightclub – but this time they were carrying guns. They came back to demand that I leave, not realising that I had already gone. When I heard about this, I was deeply disturbed – I mean, they had come back carrying weapons, who knows what could have happened if Michael and I had still been there. Their hatred for me ran that deep. But hatred for what? It wasn't as if they actually knew me. They just knew of me.

The cumulative effect of these nightclub incidents was that I became incredibly anxious when put into these kinds of situations. Going out became something I would dread, rather than look forward to; I began to associate clubs with fear. Instead of my fame bringing people to me in a positive way, it was beginning to be an albatross around my neck. Rather than people coming up to me and being pleased to see a famous face, they resented seeing me because of my fame – it was all back to front. I started to dread the thought of going out and as a result actively avoided it – and ended up living like a recluse, terrified of my own shadow.

Even now, I dread the thought of going out to a nightclub; I still associate it with trouble and fear. If Kate suggests going to a club, my stomach ties itself in knots as I begin to anticipate the worst before it has even happened. You would have thought that, by now, I would have got over the issue, but it haunts me to this day.

Many times while I was in Sydney I rang my good friend

George back home on the Gold Coast and cried down the phone to him. I daren't tell my brothers what was happening to me because I knew they'd be on the first plane and war would break out once they got their hands on the gangs who were giving me grief.

One night a group of kids spotted George in a club and recognised him as my mate. They pulled him into the toilet and held a knife to him, saying, 'Tell us where Andre is or we'll cut your throat!'

Most people would have been so scared they would have split on their grandmother. But not George. He said, 'If you're going to slice my throat you may as well do it because I would never tell you where he is.' Then he spat in their faces and got a severe beating for it. He was the kind of friend who was willing to die for you and that's why we remain so close to this day. You can trust certain people with money – you can trust them with your girlfriends even – but can you trust them with your life? With George, I can.

One of the worst death threats came before one of my Bobby Brown shows. Some nutter had cut out words from a newspaper to write the icy message: 'When the colour turns blue, watch the light and watch who's watching you. Death awaits.' (I know, like something out of *The Bodyguard*, right?)

I took it to the police, who said it was nothing to worry about. But, as the concert drew near, I took a call from a detective who said there could be something in it after all. It seemed similar threats had been received by support bands in America, and in some cases there had been violence. That was just what I needed!

'Gimme Little Sign' contains the lines:

When you're feeling blue an' I want you
There's just one thing you should do.

And then the music stops, before the lyrics go on, after a pause of a second or two:

Just gimme a little sign, girl.

The way the police figured it, at the point when the music stopped, the nut would shoot me. It was only a theory, of course, but they didn't want to take any chances because of all the trouble that was going on in Sydney at that time between Greek, Italian and Lebanese gangs, so they urged me not to do the show. But there was no way I wasn't going on stage, so they sent 26 police to the arena to protect me. The audience probably thought Bobby needed the extra security.

The police were at the side of the stage and in front of it. What they thought they could do if someone pulled a gun, I couldn't imagine. But it felt reassuring to know they were there. In a way I almost convinced myself that I would be shot that night, and stupidly I thought, What a way to go. At least I'll be remembered as a performer. Once again I was putting my career before my life. My priorities were so, so wrong.

Anyway, as you've guessed, the big song came round and I gave it my best. What else can you do when, in the back of your mind, you think this may be the last number you ever perform? The blue spotlight was on me, and when the music stopped I suppose I should have held my breath and waited for the fatal shot but, in reality, I was enjoying the moment far too much to think about anything else at all. It seemed like an eternity before I realised that the moment had been and gone and I was still alive and kicking. But I wasn't sure how much more I could take of all this.

I was starting to go out less and less. Whenever I did go to a club, I'd always have to bring along loads of security. Every time I went to a club I expected to get into a major fight, have a knife put to my throat or a bottle smashed on my head. Every time there was some kind of threat I started to fear for my life.

As it turned out, I was no longer living a pop dream; I was living a nightmare. Suddenly I started to hate Australia and what it was doing to me. I went from being on the cover of every magazine to being the butt of jokes. I had this dreadful long hair which people loved to poke fun at. I hated my life. I hated Australia, and most of all I hated the record industry for doing this to me. Looking back now, I realise what I actually hated was myself. It wasn't Australia's fault or the record industry's fault. I just took it all far too seriously. But then a lifeline came. The record company decided to send me to England to write another album for the Australian market. I was so relieved because here was my escape.

CHAPTER FOUR

RIPPED AND TONED

WHEN I FINISHED the Madonna tour in December 1994, I took a few days out to rest, then boarded a plane to London. Apart from my relatives, no one in Britain knew of my success Down Under. I had wanted so much to make it in my native country ever since I was signed up by Melodian/ Mushroom, who had a tiny office in the King's Road in London. At first the label wanted me to concentrate on writing the album, but once I had a few tracks under my belt they started to book a few personal appearances in Britain for me.

The money was pathetic – £10 and pay for your own petrol – but it was what I wanted. That first gig was amazing. The crowd didn't know me from Adam but by the end of the evening they were going ballistic. Naturally a report on my success got back to the record company, so they decided to push it a bit further. We created little cards to give out at personal appearances which said, 'If you want more information about Peter Andre write to this address.' At first the letters arrived in their hundreds. Then thousands. Then tens of thousands. Mushroom knew they had a hit on their hands, and for me a dream was starting to come true.

I was booked into a string of what I call teen clubs. They open at nine o'clock in the evening, no one over 16 is allowed in, and they don't serve alcohol. The response was wild. Even at my peak in Australia it had never been like this. I didn't know what hysteria was until I came to England. They loved the songs I'd had hits with in Australia and the new ones I'd been writing for the album. My dancing had also improved a lot because of the amount of work I'd been putting in, and I had some tremendous dancers with me.

Mushroom gradually worked their way through the avalanche of letters from fans and told me that they would need at least 20,000 names on their database before they could consider releasing a record in Britain. The figures turned out to be many times bigger than that, so it was time for the Andre career to move up a gear. We did a video for a song called 'Turn It Up', my first British release. That was in June 1995 and the single reached a modest 64 in the charts.

One of the early gigs I did was on the Isle of Wight, as part of the *Mizz* magazine roadshow, and backstage I met a woman named Claire Powell, who was in business with another woman, Sue Harris, at Blitz Management. Halfway through a song I looked offstage and saw Claire, her jaw hanging down, nudging Sue and shouting in her ear. When

I walked off, Claire rushed up to me and said, 'Your performance was fantastic. I've been speaking to Helen at Mushroom and I'm interested in managing you.'

'Oh, thank you,' I said in a strange tone, a bit shocked by her approach.

'No, you don't understand,' she carried on. 'I see the potential – you have to let me manage you.'

No one had put that kind of faith in me before. I couldn't believe it – how could this woman be so committed on the strength of just one performance? I said I'd think about it – I wasn't going to rush in like I had with Molly – and suggested she speak to my dad. Claire kept calling over the next few days, urging me to sever my ties with Australia and sign up with her.

It took one heck of a lot of courage for me to phone Molly and tell him. Even though he was 12,000 miles away, I was still overawed by him because he was so damn powerful in the music industry. Eventually I made the call and told him that I had found someone in England who wanted to look after my professional interests there. To my amazement, he was so cool about it. Things were starting to happen really quickly. Suddenly the organisers of the *Mizz* roadshow were moving me higher up the bill. Sean Maguire had been headlining, but it soon became obvious that all the kids were leaving straight after my performance to come and wait backstage.

Blitz spoke to Gary Ashley and Nina Frickberg at Mushroom UK and Claire convinced them that the quickest way to make me a star would be to take me on a school tour. By now my fan base was growing by 4,000 a week.

Mushroom weren't keen on investing in me, but Claire is a mighty persuasive lady who doesn't take no for an answer. Thank God she doesn't, for that school tour made me. I was only the second artist to do such a tour and we went to hundreds of schools around the country.

Every morning I was getting up at 6am, ready to perform in the morning assembly at 9am. Afterwards I'd do a Q&A session with the kids. I warned them about the pitfalls of the music industry and the dangers of drugs. Because I've always enjoyed public speaking, I loved those sessions. Then we would go straight into doing regional press or radio and frequently another performance in the afternoon. Often I'd perform a third gig in the evening at an under-18s club. I was exhausted.

We were staying in really grotty hotels and eating whatever we could find. I remember this one hotel in Ireland with pink and orange bedspreads and dirty lace curtains. These were the sorts of places you might see in an American heist movie. The travelling was gruelling and the money was rubbish, but I found the hard graft exhilarating. Although life on the road was tough, I never complained. I knew this was what I wanted and watching the fan base grow was incredible. Eventually there were so many kids blocking the car parks, I had to hire a security guard, my brother Danny.

A couple of years earlier, back in Australia, I'd met a London band called East 17. We all got on really well and Brian Harvey had said to me, 'If you ever come to England I'll personally put you on a tour with us.' As my school tours drew to a close, Claire rang up the band's manager, Tom Watkins, and reminded him of Brian's promise. Tom wouldn't hear of it, so Claire rang Brian directly and he was delighted with the idea. He managed to persuade Tom to change his mind and we struck a deal. I had to pay for the privilege of appearing on the bill with East 17 but it was worth every penny. I knew Tom wasn't convinced, but I thanked him for letting me be on the tour.

But I had the satisfaction of proving him wrong. I opened for East 17 all over the country and the tour was a huge success. It was the Peter Andre launchpad. I'll always thank Brian, Tony, Terry and John for their belief in me – especially Brian.

For days I lived in the Rollover Studios in Beethoven Street in west London, sleeping on the couch and writing round the clock to get the album finished. Looking back, I'm not sure if the record company were just letting me write for months so that I'd be off their backs or whether they knew I'd produce the goods if I was given enough time.

I was working with a producer called Ollie Jacobs on a track which would eventually become 'Mysterious Girl'. One night, after we'd been writing for hour after hour, I told everyone to leave the room. We'd already changed it hundreds of times and everyone was tired. But then, as if by magic, Ollie hit upon the right chords and a hit was born.

When it first came out, 'Mysterious Girl' did what 'You Drive Me Crazy' had done three years earlier. It went in at number 53 but not because it was a bad song; it was just the wrong time of year for something so bouncy and summery. Not only that, I hated the video they had made to promote it. I begged Mushroom UK to give me an editing suite and an editor so that I could do my own cut of the video. I even offered to pay for it myself, but fortunately Claire convinced them to let me use a suite, so they didn't hold me to that. For 48 hours straight we sat in the edit suite and, piece by piece, turned the 'Mysterious Girl' video into what I knew in my heart would sell the record. It was all my own work and I was so proud of it. I still am.

At first the record didn't do too well on its second outing in Britain. But then it started to play on a TV show called *The Box*, in which viewers voted for their favourite video. Nearly all the top 30 videos were American, but among those that weren't was mine. And the more times it was played the more people voted for it and drove it up the chart. Eventually, in May 1996, it got to number one and stayed there.

After 'Mysterious Girl' had failed the first time out, I released a song called 'Only One' which I'd also written with Ollie Jacobs. It went in at number 16, which to me was a miracle. I even did *Top of the Pops* and you can imagine how proud I was to ring my mum to tell her that her little boy was making it big back in Britain. Even though I was thrilled to have been on the show, the performance was not great – and my styling was dreadful!

On the strength of 'Only One' and the success of my school tour, I was asked to be the support act for Boyzone on their 1996 tour. It just kept getting better for me. By the time of the first Boyzone gig, the 'Mysterious Girl' video had been number one on *The Box* for three weeks running, the first time that had ever happened to a British act. By the end of the Boyzone tour it had been number one on the TV show for 12 weeks and had gone straight into the singles charts at number three. At last the big offers started coming in and this time it wasn't £10 a performance but more like £10,000. The overnight change was unbelievable. 'Mysterious Girl' sold about 900,000 copies and was the biggest-selling single of the year.

Surprisingly, though, it never hit number one until I left the jungle eight years later, after *I'm A Celebrity Get Me Out Of Here!* and re-released it in 2004. Back in 1996 Bryan Adams had his marathon number-one stint with '(Everything I Do) I Do It for You'. 'Mysterious Girl' stayed locked at number two and neither single would budge. Then Mushroom pulled a master stroke. They decided that, if we took the record out of the shops and released another one, this new record would cash in on the demand for 'Mysterious Girl' and sell enough to go into the charts at number one. And what do you know, it did! The song was 'Flava'. The pre-sales alone were a quarter of a million.

But, as my success grew, so did my workload, and the cracks were beginning to show. We filmed the video for 'Flava' on Venice Beach in Los Angeles. Obviously my record company thought I deserved a bit more than a dingy studio in London. But we only had three days, including the flights, to do the shoot, so the pressure was really on. Over the past few months I'd become fixated on America. I ordered loads of baggy clothes and baseball caps for the shoot and even started to talk with an American accent. I must have sounded like a right idiot!

Part of the reason why the 'Mysterious Girl' video had been so successful was because the public were obsessed by men with abs. They weren't the only ones! I was desperate to look right in the video and woke up at 4.30am just so I could go to the gym before we started shooting. I refused to eat anything. It was a scorching day and I'm surprised I even managed to dance in those temperatures. Every time we broke from filming, I'd run into the shade to do my sit-ups. Claire thought I was crazy.

'*Please* eat something, Peter,' she begged me. 'You're going to pass out if you carry on like this.'

'Yeah, yeah,' I said, waving her away. 'I'll eat later. I need to look ripped for the video.'

Eventually, around 2pm, I agreed to eat some fish. We'd rented a house in Beverly Hills for the shoot and needed to arrive for sunset. We were so far behind schedule that we didn't even get there until 8pm. The sun would be setting at 8.10pm and I had eight minutes to get ready. It was crazy, but we did it.

We didn't finish shooting until 3am. Immediately after we'd wrapped, I started to feel terrible.

'Pete, are you OK?' asked Claire. 'You look really white.'

All of a sudden I felt acid rising uncontrollably in my stomach, and before I knew it I was projectile vomiting in front of everyone, all over the place. It was such a mess. Everyone was concerned and Claire rushed me to a doctor. It turned out I was suffering from exhaustion and dehydration.

The next day I was due to fly to Glasgow for two really important AIDS benefit concerts with Boyzone. The doctors in the US had given me several injections and said it would be impossible for me to fly. Claire flew back without me and

I was forced to cancel the first night. A story leaked out that I was suffering from a mystery illness and the press went nuts. The rumours flying around were ridiculous and some papers even reported that I was dying. I flew back to Britain the next day and arrived at the venue covered in a cloak. After the show Claire took me aside and had a serious talk with me. I needed to calm down, she said. In return she agreed to set aside proper time in my schedule for training and eating.

I've always had an addictive personality. For the most part my obsessions are healthy, although they do occasionally spiral out of control. I've never been tempted by drugs, but I do have one big weakness – strong, strong coffee! For a long time I never touched the stuff. I was doing a promotional tour of European territories and my interview schedule was gruelling. I'd wake up at 7.15am and my first interview would be at 7.45. I wouldn't stop all day. I was losing concentration and I felt tired. Then some French guy said, try one of these. It was espresso. No chance, man, I told him. But then I took a shot and I was on fire. And so coffee became my new addiction. I started to love the social aspect of having a coffee. I was fascinated with the whole culture. I went through all the different beans. I was a coffee slave – I still am!

During this time I was still feeling confused about life and what I wanted, but I was determined never to go back to Australia. Even though I was thousands of miles away, I couldn't help but keep looking over my shoulder, always in fear of those gangs who had made my life a misery. In the daytime I'd be the happiest man in the world, but as soon as it started to get dark I felt threatened. Don't get me wrong, I loved Australia, it is Paradise on earth; but I was scarred – deeply scarred.

For a long time practice, training, girls and drink became my only outlets. I drank heavily at home and I could get through several bottles of wine with ease. With me in Britain and Kathy in Australia, we were drifting further and further apart. How else could it go? So on the phone I began hinting to Kathy that, unless she moved over to England, she and I just weren't going places any more. She was a ballet teacher and had her own school, so her reaction was understandable: 'Why do I have to go to England? Why can't you come back here? Is your career more important than mine?' I was trying slowly, so slowly, to break it off but I didn't want to see her with someone else. I was so selfish.

Very soon one infidelity led to another and this was the beginning of a very bad period. I started sleeping with many many girls. To this day I don't know how many I've slept with and it's become the subject of many arguments between me and Kate. I went nuts for mixed-race girls. I'd lock myself in a room with a girl and we'd have sex for days. But it was never love. I even went so far as to deck my bed out with black satin sheets and pillows – how sad is that? For starters you slide off those pieces of shit. I wouldn't sleep between them now if you paid me! I created my own den with dim lighting, champagne and music. I was a bad boy.

I've been with married women, single women, older women – I just couldn't get enough of women! It was stupid.

I feel disgusted when I picture these situations and think how close I came to being caught indulging my own stupid selfish pleasures.

If there's one piece of advice I could give, it's stay away from married people. You don't know the damage you do. Of the Ten Commandments, I was breaking at least five. When I look back I think, Was I really like that? It's not something I'm proud of. I had no respect for these girls or myself. I was rebellious and sex became my only release. If I'm honest with myself, I was feeling very lost and lonely. The more I felt like that the more I did it. Sex was my drug and I was addicted. I needed both the attention and the control. But I never, ever went with a girl who didn't want to be with me 100 per cent. My sense of power came from the fact they wanted it so badly that I could take control.

I've always been the type who wanted to get married and have kids – always. I was waiting for the one. At that time I didn't have the willpower. Now I no longer need willpower because I'm with the most beautiful woman in the world. There was only one other girl in my past that I would have considered spending the rest of my life with and we didn't even sleep together. Her name was Laura Vasquez.

I met Laura when I went back to Australia to perform on *Steve Vizard*, a TV show along the lines of David Letterman's. In the next studio they were filming *Home and Away*. Laura (who played Sarah) and Melissa George (who played Angel) both came to watch my performance. Laura was clearly impressed. Afterwards, she told me she'd always wanted to meet me. She was Argentinean and I remember thinking she looked really cute. For some time we texted each other and after I flew back to England we stayed in touch. Then, whenever we were in the same country, we would always meet up. I loved Laura as a mate, but I didn't look at her any differently until one day I woke up and it hit me that I really, really liked her.

But even throughout my period of unfaithfulness, I never cheated on Kathy with Laura. I liked Laura and I didn't want to disrespect her by taking her virginity. That's really important to me, because I've never been with a virgin to this day. If you take that from someone, you have to be prepared to commit properly. Laura and I fell for each other. Her mum was the sweetest person and we used to ring each other to talk about Laura. She even translated one of my songs into Spanish for me.

Laura was as consistent as Kate would be in later years; every day she would ask me, 'Do you want to be with me? Let's make it happen.'

Eventually, she gave up. I really did like her but I don't think she ever understood my motivations. I simply felt she was too good to be messed about and at that point in my life I didn't trust myself. Then, towards the end of my relationship with Kathy, I actually believed I was ready to commit to Laura. 'Look, I'm ready. I know it,' I told her over the phone.

'But you've said this to me before,' she said. 'You've strung me along.'

For the next two weeks I poured my heart out, but it was too little too late. Laura had since started seeing Kingsley from the group MN8.

'You lied to me,' I cried. 'At least I never lied to you!'

She was so hurt. Her mum called me and said, 'Peter, she didn't believe you. That's why she started seeing Kingsley.'

I didn't speak to Laura for about six months. Then, after another year, I heard she was married and I was devastated. My heart was broken and I couldn't help but think it must be karma. But to be honest, I'm glad she didn't wait because I wouldn't have changed her life. I saw her again a couple of years later, but it was hard because our feelings for each other were so strong. She told me, 'It will break my heart when I hear about you getting married, but I know it's going to happen.'

I don't want Kingsley to think I met up with Laura secretly. It was nothing like that. I bumped into her. Out of respect for her and her husband I stayed away. The next thing I heard, she had a child and I was really proud of her. Once she'd had the child I let go. Before I met Kate, I thought Laura was the one.

Thankfully, Kate is the only girl I've ever made pregnant. Bizarrely, for a long time I found it almost impossible to climax in girls. At first I thought it was a blessing, but eventually I went to the doctor about it. I was told that I was so in control of my mind that I refused to let go. But it never happened with Kate. I must have had so much love. She has that touch for me. I can just kiss her, touch her face or hold her hand a certain way and it gets my pulse racing. I know that's got to be love. I've never felt that way before, which is probably why our lovemaking is so ridiculously and unbelievably passionate. There are so many times we don't want to have sex; we want to make really intense love.

Despite my personal problems, my professional life was really exciting. I performed at the World Music Awards in Monaco, where I met Lionel Richie, Celine Dion and Halle Berry for the first time. It was 1997 and 'I Feel You' had just gone to number one in Britain. This was the first time I'd ever performed in front of this calibre of artists and also my first real taste of luxury. We were booked into the Hotel de Paris and I couldn't believe the size of the rooms, the gyms and the swimming pool. During the day we were taken out on speedboats and at night I mixed with bigwigs at the yacht club.

Halle Berry was my dream woman with that lovely coffee-coloured skin but my legs were shaking as I stood next to her and I was so nervous I couldn't speak. Dave Hogan from the *Sun* took a photograph of us and I begged Claire to get hold of a copy. Finally, she did and it appeared in the programme for my Arena Tour.

I was staying in a block of apartments on London's Old Brompton Road, just behind Earl's Court. Ant and Dec were living directly above me and Danni Minogue was living next door. We were always throwing parties, but there was a rivalry between myself and Ant and Dec because I was quickly moving up the ranks. They were great though – good old PJ and Duncan! – and I do thank them for what they did in the jungle – they even took the piss in a nice way, and they helped me a lot.

By now I was mixing with a music-industry crowd, but this time they were much bigger names than I'd ever been with before. The first person who gave me a drag of what I innocently thought was a cigarette was Mick Hucknall. I don't know what it was laced with, or whether he knew it was laced, but that night I almost ended up in hospital. It was rolled up like a joint but he told me it was a ciggie. I took a couple of big drags to try to look cool and before I knew it I was hallucinating. I started to hear sirens and I thought I was going to pass out. On the way home I told my good mate Dean Stratton from Mushroom to take me to the hospital. But I didn't blame Mick, because it was my own stupid fault. I'm not sure if anyone else at the party noticed; or maybe they just thought I was a bit strange.

My second encounter with cigarettes took place in 1998 when I was on a promotional tour with All Saints in Europe. We were in a club and I asked Melanie Blatt if I could have a drag on her cigarette. I'd always quite fancied Melanie. She looked at me stunned, then laughed and asked, 'Have you ever had a cigarette?'

All of a sudden I felt peer pressure. I wanted to look really cool in front of all the girls and I just ended up looking stupid. But from that night on I was a smoker – for a while.

Mel and I had been seeing each other for a while years earlier, before she and Shaznay teamed up with Nicole and Natalie. It lasted six months, but I was a lot more serious about her than she was about me. Funnily enough, we never made love. She was going through a hard time at that point. I'm disgusted by my behaviour now, but I acted like a complete arsehole. I thought she didn't want to make love to me because I didn't turn her on. I kept on hassling her. In the end she said, 'If you can't just be with me for me, then...'

And so I left her. I bumped into Melanie seven years ago and she told me how much I'd hurt her. People used to say I could have anyone I wanted but that's rubbish – no one can. When you think you can have anyone you want, you won't believe how many people suddenly can't stand you. I'd already rejected my fair share of girls, and the tables would soon turn.

CHAPTER FIVE

ON THE ROAD

WITH 'MYSTERIOUS GIRL' so big in Britain, the record company asked me to go back to Australia to promote it there. Abuse was my first thought and I could think of nothing worse. The idea of it made me feel sick because of everything I'd suffered there. Believe me, the memories were still so raw and painful. But I had to go back, however much I hated the prospect of being threatened and abused by people in the streets.

Throughout the flight my nerves were jangling and when we'd landed and I was waiting to go through passport control I felt sick, sweaty and horrible. And it wasn't from the heat. I had my hat pulled right down over my face and all I could think was, Please, I don't want to get noticed, I don't want to get abused. No more threats from the public, please. I hated every minute of it.

I also had a lot on my mind about what was going on back in England. I had heard mutterings at Mushroom UK before

'Mysterious Girl' came out that they were planning to drop me because they didn't think I would come up with the goods. Gary Ashley had left, Nina Frickberg had moved on and Korda Marshall had taken over. Everything was crumbling behind the scenes. Then 'Flava' saved me by going to number one.

Gary and Nina had been the key to my success at Mushroom Records. Now there was a whole new team that didn't have the same vision. They gave the impression of wanting to ride on the back of the success I'd had, without putting the money or the marketing behind me to create more hits. The night 'Flava' topped the charts I sat in my room, so depressed that it was all I could do to hold back the tears. That's how hard it hit me that I was being sent back to Australia. I was petrified at that prospect, and at the same time I was very worried that my career might not go the way I wanted in Britain.

The label's new boss and I didn't see eye to eye at all. After 'Flava' I wanted to do 'I Feel You', a ballad which would show off my vocal ability. After a lot of arguments between me and Mushroom, they agreed – and I had the second number one in a row, thanks to Claire helping me to push for this.

One of the media people who really went for 'I Feel You' was Dominic Mohan, who was running the Bizarre column in the *Sun*. He came out to Los Angeles with Dave Hogan, the showbiz photographer, and we all got on unbelievably well for three days. I've always liked Dave, who is one of the nicer photographers, but Dominic and I would have a behind-the-scenes dislike for each other for years. In LA we did shoots by the pool, talked about the music I liked and went out to dinner, and he was great. I thought I'd made a real friend.

Dominic said, 'You're a really nice guy and people are going to be shocked to know what you're really like.' Then at the end of the third day, just before he was due to head for the airport, he dropped one on me.

'Hey, we haven't talked about sex,' he said.

'Dominic, you know I'd rather just talk about music.'

'Come on, we've got to have at least one small comment about sex.'

'Well, what do you want to know?' I asked reluctantly.

'How many women have you slept with?'

'Oh, man, I'm not gonna say that,' I told him. I was 24 and the nice guy in pop. I didn't want to look like a sleazebag.

So I gave him a five-minute description of my sex life and that's what made the headlines. I was gutted, because so much of my career was based on image and I didn't want it tarnished. From then on I argued with Dominic and he argued with me. He killed me in the press and maybe I deserved it. I found it character-building and Dominic and I recently buried the hatchet. I thanked the bastard for giving me a rude awakening. Today I don't mind admitting my past. I feel free now.

It was while making the 'I Feel You' video that I met a girl from Brixton called Charlene Ediland. She was half-Jamaican and half-Swedish and at that point in my life she was the most beautiful woman I'd ever seen. With her green eyes, brown hair and light coffee-coloured skin, she was stunning.

Charlene was the leading lady in the video. I chose her myself because the moment I met her at the audition I was crazy about her. It was a weird kind of relationship, because I was obsessed with her. I'd never felt that way with a girl before.

She became everything. I didn't want to go to work, I just wanted to be with her all the time. I don't believe it was love – I know because I'm in love with Kate. Being in love is not wanting to be away from someone, or feeling unable to function without that person being there; not in an obsessive way, though, but more in the sense that they complete you. Kate and I have to be together every night – not because I'm scared she'll leave me for someone else – but because I need her to feel complete. That's how I know what love is now.

I didn't feel complete with Charlene. I didn't want anyone to set eyes on her except for me. It got to the point where I didn't even want her to work. She was working as a bar girl and often wore see-through dresses. I hated it. It was really wrong and it drove her to insanity.

Oddly, Kate was the one girl I said I'd never trust and yet she's the only one I've ever trusted. I know a lot of that is because I'm happy with myself and I trust myself. But I'd been unfaithful for so long that when Charlene came along I assumed she'd be doing it to me. After six months together I was convinced she was seeing someone else. It was killing me and I've never known the truth. But, looking back, I don't blame the girl. I never cheated on her, never even thought about it. But I was too gone – and it was wrong.

Perhaps because I'd already lost girls like Laura and Mel

Blatt, I felt I needed someone I could hold on to. I wanted her to be on tour with me because I didn't want her out of my sight. An obsession like that is unhealthy. My head was always hurting when she wasn't with me because I was constantly wondering who she was with, who she was talking to, who she was looking at and who was looking at her.

We were on tour, doing 30-odd dates all across Europe, when I decided I couldn't take it any more. We slept together after each show but, unusually, we didn't do anything that night, and when we woke in the morning I looked into those big green eyes, drew a deep breath and told her, 'It has to end. You've got to go.'

It sounds brutal now, but I felt it was easier to just come out with it. She was shocked and we both cried, but we knew it was the right thing to do. All day I was a wreck. I couldn't face anyone, couldn't talk to anyone. For the remainder of that tour I refused to perform 'I Feel You'. It brought back too many memories. I couldn't listen to the song for about a year; it absolutely killed me. It took a long time to get over Charlene; in truth, years. When I watch the video now, I have good memories, but that is because I am with someone I really love, Katie, and my emotions are rock-solid.

It was in the midst of my relationship with Charlene that I finally split up with Kathy. She rang me one day when I was in the shower and Charlene picked up the phone.

'Who are you?' Kathy said.

'I'm Peter's girlfriend,' replied Charlene.

'That's funny, I am too,' said Kathy, then burst into tears. Later she called again and this time I made sure I got to the phone first. Kathy was still bawling her eyes out and shouted, 'You arsehole. Why couldn't you have just told me?'

'I've been trying to tell you for the last couple of years,' I said.

But I knew I was wrong to have treated her so badly. She was right – I was an arsehole. But I got my comeuppance, as you always do when you mess around with people's emotions.

While I didn't want to be in Australia any more, I wasn't sure I wanted to be in England either. I no longer felt Mushroom really believed in me. I was exhausted. I'd just finished a regional tour of 2,000-seat venues. My management had hired me a helicopter to help promote the dates and the whole tour sold out within one day. It was a great success, but I couldn't help feeling that I needed a break. Something inside was nagging at me. Cracking America had always been my dream and every day I grew more obsessed with releasing a record there. Eventually, at the end of 1996, Claire agreed I deserved some time off and we flew to LA.

Those first few weeks were spent living in the Sofitel Hotel, opposite the Beverly Center. Thinking back, I must have caused Claire a real headache. Not only did I demand our hotel should have a gym, but I also insisted on very particular weights. She searched high and low for hotels with the right equipment. It was the same throughout the whole early part of my career. The Sofitel had a 24-hour gym and I remember being really impressed, and Mike and I trained our arses off. At the time I was so selfish. All I thought about was what I needed, what I wanted. Nobody else mattered. I still can't believe Claire stuck with me throughout that period. She put up with a lot and I'm eternally grateful for her loyalty.

After a month at the Sofitel, I got back to the hotel one day to find my belongings had been packed away.

'We need to move to another hotel,' said Claire, her suitcases already packed.

'But why? What's wrong with this place?' I complained, tired after a long day in the studio. In fact, there was a lot wrong. I was sick and tired of living in hotels. It was all I'd done for the past few years, and I was desperate for my own apartment.

After checking out of the Sofitel, we jumped into a cab and rode across town. I had no idea where Claire was taking us. I certainly didn't expect the plush Beverly Hills mansion we pulled into.

'What's going on?' I said, confused.

'This is your new home, Peter,' smiled Claire.

Without my knowing, she had gone out and found us a house to rent for the next few months. It was such an incredible place. There were six bedrooms, a Jacuzzi, a pool, a steam room and even a koi pond in the garden. I couldn't believe it. I was like a little kid running between all the rooms. Claire had even cooked a roast dinner to be ready when I arrived – it was the one thing I was really missing about England and I'd been moaning about it for the past few weeks. Even better, I could smell fresh waffles in the oven. I'd never allow myself to eat food like that on tour, but every now and then I'd relax a bit.

Then the strangest thing happened. Claire was carrying a

plate of food from the kitchen, when suddenly she let out a piercing scream.

'What's happened?' I said, running over to her.

'Ow, my foot,' she cried, holding on to her toe.

I looked closely and her foot had swollen to the size of a football.

'That's a scorpion bite,' I said. I'd seen plenty back home in Australia and it was unmistakable.

'Don't be ridiculous,' tutted Claire. 'We're in Beverly Hills – not the outback!'

But I knew I was right. I was convinced the scorpion must still be somewhere in the house. Me, Mike and Dean started scanning the floor, lifting up cushions, rummaging through papers. I refused to give up. By now Claire had broken into a sweat and her face looked really pale. Paul Domaine, my choreographer, was with Claire in the kitchen.

'I'm gonna call 911,' I said.

Luckily the ambulance arrived in minutes. And guess what I found behind the TV? A scorpion. It was the first reported sighting in Beverly Hills in 50 years!

But that was just the first of several weird occurrences. The next day we flew to Arizona to film my 'Lonely' video. It was a scorching day and 49°C in the shade. It was so hot you could fry an egg on the rocks – so we did, honest!

'What are the chances of it raining here?' I joked to our location scout.

'Rain here? Impossible. It hasn't rained in 50 years,' he replied.

But, as the afternoon went on, we noticed several grey clouds were gathering. Before long the area was having one of its freakiest storms to date. Even hail was falling. We had a plane to catch that evening, so we all jumped in the back of a Winnebago and sped along the highway. There was thunder and lightning the whole way. I really thought I was going to die out there on the road. I even phoned my mum and dad!

When we eventually boarded the plane we were told almost immediately to get off. For the first time ever at that airport, a plane had been struck by lightning. I couldn't believe it. We were convinced it must be Claire.

'You're jinxed!' I told her.

It's become an ongoing joke with us. Now, whenever Kate and I go away, we always tell Claire she's not coming! (We still love you though... jinx.)

During those months in Beverly Hills my writing really improved. I'd work late every night in the studio and enjoy lie-ins every morning. It was bliss. On days off, me and Mike would bring the TV and DVD player outside, lay by the pool and watch gangster movies.

In June 1997 I flew back to Britain for my Arena Tour. Claire and I were determined it would be the best show on earth. To say it was spectacular is an understatement. A few months earlier Claire had taken me to see the Cirque du Soleil in Las Vegas and I was determined to use some of the show's ideas in my tour. All my outfits were designed along a Judge Dredd theme and the stage was set to look like a dark American backstreet. I've always prided myself on being a great entertainer and that's something no one can take away from me. Even during the preparations for my and Kate's wedding, I was responsible for most of the entertainment – organising it, that is, not performing!

The pinnacle of the tour – and possibly my whole career – was the show at Wembley Arena. I'll never forget it. I'd only ever played at the venue as a support artist. Now it was my turn to take the main dressing room with the big bathroom. For at least an hour before the show no one was allowed to disturb me. I even made my road manager, Nigel, stand guard outside the door.

I'd developed a strict routine on tour and would go nuts if it was ever disrupted. First I'd drink hot water with honey and do my vocal training, next I'd pump up my chest and abs and finally I'd get dressed. I always refused to eat before a show and would only ever have a light lunch that day. As soon as I came off stage I'd be starving. I'd often rush on to the tour bus and pull out a plastic container filled with pasta and chicken which had been prepared earlier. It had to be that exact dish, prepared in that exact way – I refused to eat anything else. I'd finish most of it before the bus had even pulled away! I'd take my own food, plus a protein drink, on flights too, to avoid what I saw as unhealthy airline meals. Looking back, I'm embarrassed at how arrogant and self-centred I'd become. I thought the world really did revolve around me.

The opening part of the show was really dramatic. My back to the audience, I was lowered on to the stage in a cage. It cost thousands of pounds in insurance to arrange, but it looked incredible. Around me I could hear rockets being launched and the piercing screams of 10,000 kids. It was ten minutes before I even moved! I was in my element. At that moment I really thought I'd arrived. Little did I know that years later I'd discover the real meaning of happiness with my wonderful wife and two sons.

The following night I went to see one of my all-time heroes, Michael Jackson, play at Wembley Stadium. I'll admit the guy was in a league way above anyone. The concert was great, but I felt very awkward and uncomfortable. It was that same sick feeling I'd had in Sydney. There were over 80,000 people in the crowd that night, but I was convinced everyone was looking at me. Who might jump on me? Who might pull a knife on me? Claire told me to stop being so ridiculous, but she didn't understand. Looking over my shoulder every five minutes, I became so uncomfortable that I demanded we leave. Over the past few months America had become my new home and safe haven. I was obsessed with dressing American and hanging out with Americans. Nothing else mattered and I was desperate to return.

I'd heard on the music biz grapevine that Montell Jordan, who wrote 'This Is How We Do It', on which I largely based 'Flava', wanted to write a song with me. At first I thought it must be a joke. Then I was sent a CD of a song he'd written called 'All About Us' and I loved it straight away. When we eventually met, it was like a dream.

Montell was a great guy – extremely tall, a good basketball player. He welcomed me into his home in South Central LA and I stayed there for almost three weeks. It was hard for me to take in: this Greek-Cypriot kid from England who lived in Australia was staying in South Central with Montell Jordan? Big names were always coming to visit Montell, and that's how I met stars like Coolio, Warren G and the Fugees. The atmosphere was inspirational and I was writing some great tracks for my *Time* album.

Montell's wife, who is a very astute and powerful businesswoman, said to me, 'We want to manage you in America. But you're gonna have to stay here.' That was absolutely fine by me. As usual, it didn't take me long to find a girl. I won't use her real name but will call her Monique. She was a dancer and she was married at the time, but that didn't stop me! Luckily, she was divorcing her husband and that meant the way was clear for us to spend a lot of time together.

Meanwhile, Montell's wife kept pressing me to sign with them, making promises that they could get me on some US tours. But I was scared to cut my ties with Claire in England, because things had been so successful there and if America didn't work out I would have nothing to go back to. Reluctantly, I told her no.

'Two years from now you'll be coming back to me wanting me to manage you,' she said.

It was hard to take. I always wanted to take on America, and I truly believe I could have had a lot of success there in the right hands, but now I'd blown it with the Jordans.

Monique and I were together for about a year and a half on and off. She had a tiny apartment and I decked it out to look absolutely amazing. But the girl turned out to be a psycho and really violent. She was once put inside for cracking a guy's skull with a baseball bat. One night she became really aggressive towards me. Quite bizarrely, if we didn't have sex she'd start getting angry and agitated. It used to put me off and I often hoped she'd be asleep when I got home.

Eventually I just said, 'Monique, I don't want to be with you – you annoy me, you bore me, your attitude sucks, all you do is complain about people and you start fights with people on the street. You're not the girl that I met.'

'You'd better get out of my motherfucking house,' she screamed back before coming towards me with a baseball bat.

The cops came and handcuffed us both. 'We want to know if you've hit her,' one said to me.

'Can you do me a favour, sir?' I said. 'Go in the house and look at the holes in the wall from her baseball bat and then put her name in the computer and see if she has a criminal record.'

'This ain't over!' she screamed at me as they took her away. 'I got motherfuckers in the hood!'

I knew she was friends with some real gangsters and I just wanted to get out of that scene. Besides, since I'd turned down his management offer, Montell was no longer talking to me. It was time to go back to England.

CHAPTER SIX

LOVE AND REGRET

THE WORD WAS that a new girl group had been formed and were about to release a single. As soon as I heard it, I knew it would be a hit. It had that catchy lyric in which they tell us what they want – what they really really want – yes, you know the song! And as soon as I saw the first picture of the group, I knew they'd be big.

At the time, 'Flava' had just gone to number one in the UK and I was about to headline a big national road tour. Someone had the great idea of putting the girls on the same bill with me – and that's how I first met the Spice Girls and how I embarked on a whirlwind romance with Mel B that was to end in tears and tantrums.

At the first gig I stood at the side of the stage watching them in action and enjoying the music and the brash way they took on the world. One of the road crew had told me, 'Mel, the dark one, fancies you', so as they came off stage I looked at her and she looked at me. There was definitely a spark there, as Mel was the dark, sexy type I was attracted to. Then she smiled and said breathlessly, 'Go on, Pete. Make my day. Give me a snog and then leave your girlfriend.'

My heart was beating really fast. I liked her instantly. I liked the way she looked, the way she moved, her personality and her body. But I didn't believe she fancied me. I thought it was just a game she was playing. For several days people would say to me, 'She really likes you', to which I would reply, 'Well, I really like her.' And so it went on, like a couple of kids in the playground afraid to make the first move.

Then came the Smash Hits Poll Winners' Party, where I was nominated for best male artist and the Spice Girls were up for best group. Geri was walking round backstage with a video camera in her hand, shooting scenes for the Spice Girls movie that was to come out later. Geri spotted me, raced across and said, 'Pete, pull your top up, show us your body.' Believe it or not, I suddenly went very shy and refused to give her a flash of the abs.

'What's the matter with you?' she said.

'Nothing.' I was trying to play it cool, with my shades on, but those Spice Girls were an intimidating lot. They didn't take no for an answer.

Geri started to take the mickey out of me in front of everyone. 'Ah, poor Pete – he doesn't want to lift his shirt up. What's wrong, are your abs fake?'

I didn't want to look any more stupid than I already did, so reluctantly I showed a little flesh. And we had a good laugh.

After Geri and I had finished mucking around with the camera, I went upstairs to my dressing room, and there was

The infamous shot that earned me the nickname 'The Body'. The public were obsessed by abs, but boy did I suffer to get that six-pack.

Above: Doing my PR bit at a press conference in Dubai.

Below: Performing in Paris in 1995 when I joined East 17 on their European tour.

Above: Conquering Blighty. Backstage with the *Mizz* roadshow dancers. As the show progressed and it became obvious that the crowds were leaving after they had seen me perform, the organisers of the roadshow moved me higher up the bill. The girl in the middle of the picture is Laura Vasquez who, for a long time, I felt was the one who got away.

Below: At Santa Monica Airport with my wonderful manager Claire, the one person in this business who I would trust with absolutely anything.

Above: The *Smash Hits* Poll Winners' Party – the night when Mel B asked me out on our first 'date'.

Below: I can't remember the names of the people in the middle of the picture, but that's Claire with Rod Stewart, and me on the far right.

Above left: Rod Stewart with his then wife Rachel Hunter. Rachel's sister Jackie helped me through my breakdown.

Above right: Shooting the 'Natural' video in Santa Monica airport.

Below: A relaxed dinner in LA with my brother Mike, my manager Claire and Dean Stratton, the man from Mushroom Records who believed in me the most.

Above: Suited and booted. Final preparations before embarking on my life-changing experience in the Aussie jungle in 2004.

Below: Rogue's gallery. A behind-the-scenes photo of the *I'm A Celebrity Get Me Out Of Here!* group before we entered the jungle.

Into the heart of darkness – the final moments before I entered the jungle. I might not look it, but I was nervous as hell.

Above: The camera never lies! Straight away there was a connection between Katie and me – an amazing feeling.

Below: Going on *I'm A Celebrity Get Me Out Of Here!* was the best decision of my career – it changed my life.

Mel C – Sporty Spice – waiting for me. 'Pete, you'd better go up and see Mel – she wants to see you,' she said.

My heart was going at a million miles an hour and I said to my brother Danny, who was doing my security, 'OK, I'm gonna go to their dressing rooms.'

'You can't do that,' he said. 'There's really tight security up there.'

I didn't care. I was hot to trot, and I breezed up to the dressing room, where a giant bouncer wouldn't let me go in, so I shouted through the door, 'Hello! It's Pete.'

'Let him in! Let him in!' the girls chorused, and the door was opened.

There was Mel blow-drying her hair, with no make-up on and not looking her best. She went bright red.

'You can't see me like this!' she screamed. And I found that vulnerability very attractive. When the barriers come down and you see the real person, not the image, that can be so much of a turn-on. And I was turned on that night.

It was obvious that Mel and I were attracted to each other. But the other Spice Girls were protecting her like big sisters.

'You'd better not hurt my mate, because she really likes you,' said straight-talking Geri.

'Don't worry,' I said. 'I'm a perfect gentleman.'

'Well, in that case,' said Mel, 'you'd better ditch your girlfriend and come to me.'

'I'm going to be in my dressing room,' I told her nonchalantly. 'Come by whenever you want.'

On the outside I was super cool. But inside I was shaking. I went back to my dressing room and sat there like an idiot, waiting for her to walk past. We both had to go on stage to rehearse, but I didn't want to miss the chance of her going past the dressing room so I could talk to her and maybe exchange numbers. Soon she strolled by and teased me by saying, 'Pete, make sure you give us your number before you go.'

She had me hooked. But, try as I might, I couldn't seem to get together with her again that day. After the Spice Girls did their number on stage they were rushed away and I blew my top in frustration. My brother copped a mouthful, even though it had nothing to do with him!

I was still angry on the drive home. 'When am I gonna see her again now?' I demanded of Danny, not that he had the vaguest clue. There was a missed call showing on my phone and I desperately hoped it was Mel. In fact, it was a message from my record plugger, Sarah Adams, at Brilliant. That company also handled the Spice Girls' promotions through Nicky Chapman, who later became a judge on *Pop Idol*.

Sarah's message was just what I wanted to hear. 'Mel B wants your phone number. But I don't know whether I should give it to her or not. I'm just gonna take the risk and give it to her. I hope you don't mind.'

Mind? I was jumping up and down on my seat yelling, 'Yeeeeeeeeeeeeeees!' Suddenly the phone rang again with another voicemail.

'Hello, Peter Andre, this is Melanie Brown and I wondered if you want to go out on a date with me.'

In the background I could hear the other Spice Girls laughing as she went on, 'Actually I want to go out on a date with you. So call me back.'

Naturally I called her back as quickly as I could (well, I

tried to wait 20 minutes to play it cool) and we made a date, the first of many. And that phone call was the first of up to 20 a day over the next few months. But our dates were always very odd. Our relationship had to be kept a secret at her insistence, and seeing her became a covert operation like something out of a spy thriller.

The Spice Girls had all done very well for themselves, and Mel had a fabulous apartment near Windsor. But I have to say I never felt comfortable there because there was always a strange feeling in the back of my mind that she was hiding something from me. On our first date there Mel hired a chef to come round and cook us dinner. It was great food, and very romantic, but I thought it was a bit over the top. She didn't need to try to impress me like that. I was used to staying in top hotels and knew all about the high life. After dinner, as you'd expect, we kissed and cuddled and then went through to her magnificent bedroom.

I lay back on her huge bed and watched with mounting excitement as she slowly peeled off her clothes. As she stood there as naked as the day she was born, all she said was, 'Right! This is me. If you don't like it, I'm sorry.'

My eyes were popping out on stalks. 'Are you serious?' I asked her.

She said nothing, so I got up off the bed, unzipped my trousers, pulled off my shirt, dropped my pants and said, 'Well, here I am. If you don't like me, I'm sorry too.'

She looked me up and down from head to toe very slowly and carefully and said, 'Well, I like you.'

'I like you more,' I told her. And we both laughed like a couple of little kids. Then we had sex. You couldn't call it making love – it was too selfish, with each of us concentrating on getting what we wanted. She wanted more all the time and I found that intimidating. Mel is the only woman who has made me feel that way in bed.

There's no doubt I was sexually attracted to her, but there was never the feeling that we could relax together and be comfortable. Everything was always so rushed and it never felt that we would be able to spend days together, just quick, secret, hurried sessions.

Mel, you really hurt me. But in a sense I was getting a taste of my own medicine. With other girls all I was interested in was getting their clothes off, getting it up and getting the hell out of there. I wanted more from Mel – I wanted her time and her caring. But she made it clear that what I was mainly going to get was wined, dined and laid.

This was the first time someone had treated me the way I had treated so many girls. It made me feel very vulnerable and the only way I could cope was to become even more attached to her in the hope that she would start to feel the same way for me. But she never did.

I lost count of the number of times we'd have sex at her place or in a hotel and within minutes she'd be looking at her watch and saying, 'Oh, you have to go. I'll get the driver to take you home.' It was as if she had something more important to do. But what really confused me was that on the way home she'd be on the phone to me 20, 30, 40 times. It was so bizarre! What I didn't know until later was that, during the time we were seeing each other, Mel had met a dancer called Jimmy Gulzar.

At that time Mel would ring me for advice on everything.

I felt totally involved in her life. On one occasion she called me in the middle of a record company dinner and said, 'We want to get rid of Geri. We can't handle her. We're trying to have a really important meeting and she's in the toilet with one of the male dancers. We f***ing hate her. She's driving me nuts.'

I remember thinking, Wow, if only the world knew about that! I was in a bubble that was about to burst. But I never sold a story. You see, there is always an unwritten rule that you do not sell each other out. Although I'm telling you now – but this is my book, so f**k it!

When the Spice Girls went on their tour of Europe, Mel and I would have to be apart for days at a time. One time, to my surprise, she invited me to go to Paris, even offering to pay for my flight and a hotel near where she and the girls were staying. I'd not been able to see the show in England because my presence might have started tongues wagging, but Paris seemed a safer bet and I jumped at the chance to go. I insisted on paying my own costs, though – I'm not a kept man.

I stayed in the most amazing hotel, where David and Victoria also had a suite. On the night of the concert I met David backstage and had my first proper chat with him. He's such a nice guy and we got on like a house on fire. After all, we had a lot in common – each of us was dating a Spice Girl. David even offered to get me free VIP tickets to Manchester United home games, but like a lemon I said, 'Thanks, mate, but I couldn't possibly put on you like that.' Later I regretted that, because my brother Chris is a Man U fanatic and would have loved a trip to Old Trafford.

Victoria was a very sweet girl, but a bit shy. No one

knows this, but her mum used to send mine all the British press cuttings about me and my mum would send her the Aussie stories about the Spice Girls. My brother Chris became friends with Victoria too. So, when a bitter feud broke out years later between Victoria and Katie, I wouldn't be drawn into it. I was a bit hurt recently when Victoria described me as 'a washed-up singer', because I've never said one word of criticism about her. Just because she and Katie have fallen out doesn't mean she should take it out on me. Her dispute with Katie is between the two of them, nothing to do with me or Becks. It was all a long time ago now, anyway.

And anyway, not so much of the 'washed-up'! That's a bit rich coming from someone who's never had a number one as a solo artist. David is an icon, but I am disappointed in Victoria. We all came from the same place, so by rights we should have all been friends.

Mel was playing me hard and that was doing my head in. She'd ring me and say, 'I need to see you. I'm gonna fly to you right now.' And she'd spend 30 grand hiring a private jet and before I knew it she'd be with me. But such was the pressure she put on me that, although the flesh was usually willing, the spirit was weak. Some nights my mind couldn't get in the right mood to do much more than kisses and cuddles.

It was a bewildering time. I found Mel physically attractive, but mentally she was leaving me cold. I convinced myself that any woman who'd spend a fortune on a private jet for cuddles must be deeply in love with me. But Mel wasn't. She even got married without my knowing about it.

It was at the Spice Girls' show in Paris, with me backstage, that Jimmy Gulzar proposed to Mel and she accepted. That night I was in my hotel room waiting for her to turn up – let's be honest, that was all I was there for – but the longer I waited the more I convinced myself that I shouldn't be there. When she finally slipped into the room my fears were justified, because she looked a bit sheepish and said, 'I can't.'

'You can't what?'

'I can't – you know.'

I should have known then that there was something seriously flawed in this relationship, but I was too blind to see. So we kissed and hugged, then parted.

Mel fell into the trap that so many do when they suddenly have a pile of money – she seemed to want power and control over people. I really did care about her during the 18 months or so that we were seeing each other, but there was no trust on her part. She'd often say to me, 'I don't believe you're just seeing me. I'm sure you're seeing other girls. Are you playing about on me?' She was always begging me to ring her, up to 20 times a day. And she would say, 'I love you so much. I can't be without you. I'm thinking about you.' But it was all just bullshit. At the same time she was professing her love for me, she went and married Jimmy Gulzar!

I always suspected there was something funny going on because Mel repeatedly insisted that we couldn't be seen out together in public. I always had to go to her house, often hidden under a blanket on the back seat of her chauffeur-driven limo. She would string me along and say it was because of the pressures of publicity, and she would gush that she was so happy to be in love with me because at last she had someone who understood how hard it was to be in the public eye in the music business. I fell for it. Who wouldn't?

I guess I let myself become a bit too dependent on Mel, and every time the phone rang I would hope it would be her voice at the end of the line. All the time I had the other Spice Girls warning me not to let Mel down. Mel C and Geri would warn me, 'Don't you hurt our friend,' and Victoria would say, 'You'd better not hurt her because she really likes you.' Yet all the while Mel was hurting me.

I came to feel intimidated by the whole affair and it preyed on my mind to such an extent that often I couldn't perform with Mel – and I don't mean sing. We could only snatch a few hours together at a time and the pressure on me to live up to her expectations and meet her demands was intense. Something felt wrong and I couldn't bring myself to make love to her.

Our relationship died one afternoon in Atlanta, Georgia, where Mel was doing a recording with Teddy Riley. She had begged me to fly out to see her and the minute we were alone in her hotel room we were tearing each other's clothes off, desperate to make love. Actually 'make love' makes it sound romantic. This wasn't loving at all.

I was well into my stride when suddenly the bedside phone rang. Before I could stop her, Mel reached out her arm and pressed a button on the phone to put the caller in speaker mode. I'm in action and she's now talking on the phone! But it got worse: the call was from her lawyer in London, who was telling her what was on the front page of the first edition of the *Sun*, which had hit the streets back home at about 10.15pm. The paper had an exclusive story saying that Mel was divorcing Jimmy Gulzar.

I couldn't believe what I was hearing. I didn't even know she was married – she'd always led me to believe I was the only man in her life. I stopped, looked down at her and said, 'You're married, Mel?'

But she was too busy talking to the lawyer and saying, 'Are you serious? Is that what it says?'

Divorce? Was I hearing right? I blew my top. 'Why didn't you tell me you were married?' I snarled. 'I'm here on top of you and you're laughing about getting a divorce. What are you doing to me?'

I got played at my own game. The player got played. I'd done it to girls a hundred times and now someone was doing it to me. And it hurt. Boy, it hurt. Before she could answer, I said, 'Hey! Listen to me, Mel. How could you do this to me?' All she could say was that the marriage didn't mean much to her and now it was over, so what did it matter? What did it matter? It almost killed me.

I rolled off her, lay back on the pillow and tried to keep the tears from my eyes. I knew it was no good getting angry again, as that would only make the heartache more intense for me. So I got off the bed, found my clothes and told her, 'I've got to go.' She didn't try to stop me, thank goodness. There was no going back for either of us. But that didn't stop her from ringing me all the time, even after I found myself a new girl.

Mel was a very good friend at a time when I really needed one, but I ended up feeling very vulnerable with her. And those months when we were together were weird. Both of us were afraid to let our affair come out into the open, so everything was kept under cover. It was all so secretive, that when she got married in England, I was in Australia and knew nothing about it!

And, although the sex with Mel was very good, let's face it, you can't build a serious relationship on sex alone. We were crazy together for a time. One night I got a phone call from her after she'd done the Royal Variety Performance, saying, 'I'm backstage and I'm about to shake hands with the Queen. But I can't f****ing wait to get out of here and come home and see you.' And then she told me in explicit terms exactly what she wanted to do with me. Thank God the Queen didn't know. Well, you do now, Your Majesty.

Mel had made me feel very special back then. But now I look at her and there is nothing between us at all. No spark, no chemistry, just a few memories. No one has given me the completeness that I now feel with Katie. Everything is right. We have the exact same likes, we have the same dislikes. Our relationship has sex in it, of course – lots of it – but it's not purely based on that. This is the first time I've ever felt that going to bed with someone and cuddling and watching the TV is as important as having sex. Well, almost, OK!?

Katie and I even share the same kind of insecurities. After we got together in the jungle, Mel phoned Kate and warned her that I was clingy and insecure. Maybe I did come across a bit paranoid and a bit insecure, because I was totally being played and I didn't understand why. I wasn't angry that Mel called Kate. In fact, I was happy because I love the comment Kate threw back at her.

'Oh, he's really insecure, is he?' she said. 'Well, so am I, so it's going to work perfectly, isn't it?'

That meant a lot to me. These days I'm not even slightly attracted to Mel. I don't hate her for anything that happened. I deserved it. But she hurt me a lot. You forgive but you never forget. I just want her to know the reason I was so insecure was because I really, really liked her. It was not like the love I feel for Kate, but I did love her.

CHAPTER SEVEN

LOSING IT

AFTER MEL I was lost and didn't know what to do. I didn't even know if I wanted the music any more. She was the final straw. On top of that, the sales for my second album, *Time*, were disappointing and it charted at 27, although 'All About Us' and 'Lonely' went top 5. When I found out, I locked myself in a room for three days. I didn't want to speak to anyone and I refused to eat. I was acting like a child. In Italy, where I was scheduled to do some promo, I wouldn't even come out of my room, leaving 8,000 fans waiting. In their frustration they smashed up part of the hotel, but I didn't care. Years later I recognise the same behaviour in Kate. It's why I really believe we are one and the same person.

The record company couldn't decide whether or not they wanted to release another album, and I was in a state of shock. How could a career go from being number-one hits with champagne all round to the icy-cold shoulder after just one small failure? The media were calling me a flop and very soon I became a joke.

Despite being played on urban radio for the first time, I had lost my hunger for success. I'd been performing since I was 16 and I was burning out. I simply wasn't excited any more. I'd done Wembley and I'd fulfilled my dream. Suddenly I became very agitated and aggressive. I didn't want to see a soul or be asked for an autograph. I didn't want to be around anyone except my family.

Claire said, 'Pete, you're heading for a breakdown.'

But I was so arrogant that I couldn't see where I was heading.

I'd started to take myself way too seriously. Everything was about *me*. It was the gym, the gym, the gym, and nothing else. Being obsessed with anything is unhealthy for you, both physically and mentally. To me, my image was everything. In all my video clips the lighting had to be perfect to show my body off to the best advantage. I became trapped in a vicious circle where the more I trained the better I thought I looked, and the better I looked the more I trained to keep it that way. There was no other artist out there doing it. The biggest danger in the music industry is to believe your own hype – and I did. Boy, did I!

I'd watch what I ate so carefully that my body fat went down to between five and three per cent (15 per cent is a much healthier level, and anything below eight per cent can be very dangerous) and I was so toned that staying in shape became my whole life. Looking good became more important to me than vocal or dance training, and that led to arguments with my record company on many occasions.

As I said earlier, I would only stay in hotels where the gym had exactly the right weights. Training was taking over my life to a point where I'd ring up my management and say, 'Why isn't the gym in the schedule today?'

'Well, Pete, you know, we've got radio interviews – we've got...'

'I don't care. I want the gym in it.'

When I was flying from Sydney to Thailand to do the 'Mysterious Girl' video, I asked one of the stewardesses if there was a place in business class upstairs where I could do some training. On the plane, while everyone's sleeping, I'm up there doing sit-ups and push-ups. How self-obsessed is that?

On the one hand I had a very fit, muscular body, but on the other, because I used to take my own food on the plane, I missed out on all the joys of flying first class or business class, where they ply you with comforting food and good wine to help you sit back, relax and while away the hours of a long flight.

But, like so many things in my life back then, I took my fitness and my image too far. I was so intent on looking my best for videos and stage performances that I would shave my chest hair and use baby oil to make my skin shine and look darker, just like body-builders do when they take part in contests. Pretty soon the press were slating me. They called me the 'baby-oiled boy' and criticised my 'greasy vanity'. And you know what? They were right.

The real trouble in those days was that everyone knew I had a great body but no one knew that I had a personality. No one took me seriously. They called me the 'singing abdominal', which I admit was quite funny. Then the Peter Andre Action Doll came out and what little credibility I had was shot to pieces. It didn't help that on the back of the box it said, 'Not suitable for children under 36 months due to small parts.' That was manna from heaven for the wise guys in the tabloids and stuck with me for a long time.

My management deal with Claire was drawing to an end and I just wanted to get away. If America and Britain were no longer right for me, then, despite all the bad memories Australia held for me, it was the only place left to go.

Dad and I had invested in a family hotel on an island off Brisbane called Bribie Island. 'Bribie' is Aborigine for 'meeting place by the water'. It was so lovely and peaceful there, with just the sun, the sea, the sand and the sky. The only access to the 27-room boutique hotel was across a little bridge, and the feeling that you were cut off from the outside world had a very calming effect on me. I decided to take three months off to be able to spend some time with my family. That night I felt truly content for the first time in my life. I was so relaxed. For the first time in ten years I didn't have to wake up to an itinerary the next day. I could take control of my life.

Then, bang – the breakdown happened.

On the third night after I arrived, my brothers invited me to the cinema. I said I'd rather stay at the resort, as I hadn't seen much of Mum and Dad over the previous couple of years. The hotel was almost empty that night, and Dad said he'd cook a great steak dinner for us. Later, as he prepared the meal, he looked at me and said, 'It's so good to have you home. Just you without all the hype. You know, just you.'

We sat down with a nice glass of Aussie Chardonnay and started to eat. I was holding a sharp steak knife in my hand when suddenly fireworks went off in my head. My hands shook and I saw horrible flashes of violence in my mind. Mum asked what was wrong and I just shrugged and said nothing. But the visions got worse and I imagined myself cutting my wrists. As I dropped the knife on to the plate with a clatter, Dad said, 'What's wrong? What's wrong?'

'Please, please leave me alone,' I blurted out, before running up to my room and bursting into tears. I had an inner rage that was horrific! Dad followed me, saw me sobbing and shaking on the bed and shouted down to Mum, 'Call the boys and tell them to come home – something's wrong.'

I was freaking out, yelling, screaming and shaking. I couldn't blot out the scenes flashing round my mind of me slicing my wrists and jumping out of windows. When they got there, my brothers only had to look at me to know I needed to be in hospital. They rushed me in and the doctor in casualty asked, 'Have you had many experiences of psychotic episodes before now?'

'What are you talking about?' I said. 'This has never happened before.'

'Have you ever thought of hurting your family?'

'Are you crazy? Why would I want to hurt my family?'

I couldn't work out what was happening to me, but whatever it was I knew it had been building up for a long time. Many factors had played a part: the way I felt abused and used in the early days of my career, the death threats, the success that came only to cruelly slip away and the desperate battle to show the world that the many rumours about me weren't true. The pressure was too much to bear, and to make it worse I had little to show for my success. Apart from my share in Mum and Dad's hotel, I had no property, not very much cash in the bank and a pile of bills from lawyers and the taxman.

This really was the night that changed my life. The doctors said I should go back to Mum and Dad's and relax, so my brothers drove me home. But I couldn't face being alone that night. I asked my brother Mike to stay in my room with me, like he did when we were kids. I really felt like a lost child.

The next morning I woke up feeling great. It was as if everything that had happened the night before had been just a bad dream. I went into the kitchen, where Dad was working, and he asked me how I felt.

'Just fantastic,' I told him.

'Thank God,' he said with a tear in his eye. 'Don't worry, son. Everything's all right.'

But by the afternoon I was worse than the night before. I started having terrible panic attacks during which my heart would pound in my chest and I'd break into a sweat. I was a mess. And it left me feeling so frustrated. I kept praying, asking, if I'm being punished for something, can I at least know what it is? Because I don't understand what I've done wrong. I went on to suffer 20 or 30 panic attacks every day for the next two years. What happens in a panic attack is that your heart starts beating really fast and you start hyperventilating. The official term for this, as I found out later, is a 'panic disorder'.

I tried to occupy myself during the day by doing chores. I would mop the floors and wipe down surfaces – all the simple things that I hadn't done for years but others had done for me. I thought that would be my therapy. In the daytime I could keep myself busy; at night, sleep became my only escape and soon I was sleeping almost 18 hours at a time.

Desperate to find someone who could put my head straight again, I consulted a series of doctors and therapists. But most of them talked in riddles that I couldn't understand. I convinced myself that maybe there was no cure for what was wrong with me and that I'd have to learn to live with it for the rest of my life. My distraught parents couldn't understand what the hell was happening to their son.

I decided my only option was to leave Australia. I couldn't go back to England, but I still had some good contacts in America and it was my only hope. I flew with my brothers Chris and Michael to New York, where I tried to set up meetings with a few record bosses to see if I could land a contract. I got an appointment to meet David Sonnenberg and the team from his DAS company who managed the Fugees, a band I'd written with before. At our meeting I just slayed them, so they offered to manage me in America. I could see a whole new successful life opening up before me. As usual, I was wrong.

Claire had always warned me about the pitfalls of breaking America.

'You'll be a little fish in a very big pond,' she told me.

But I refused to listen. When I chose to cut ties with Claire,

I hurt her deeply. Not only had she invested a lot of her own profits in my stage show, she'd also invested a lot of time. Leaving Claire for three years remains one of my greatest regrets to date.

I hadn't been in New York long when Claire rang me from London to tell me Disney were re-releasing *The Little Mermaid* and wanted me to record 'Kiss The Girl' for the film's soundtrack. It was while making the video that I met Gillian Wong, a half-Chinese and half-English girl who played the little mermaid. At first she acted a little snobbishly towards me, but we sat down and shared a Mars bar after the shoot. It was one of the happiest days I'd had in years and I didn't want the video to end. I hadn't worked in almost a year and it felt good to be back in front of a camera again.

Gillian and I hung out as friends for some time before our relationship became sexual. Mel was still calling me frequently, but I was heartbroken, pissed off and I didn't want to know. I was in a very vulnerable state. I was with Gillian, on and off, for 18 months. We were top mates, with no strings attached. Then one day we went out to dinner to celebrate her birthday and she wore the most incredible outfit. That night we enjoyed very wild and passionate sex. I woke up the next morning with a lot of feelings for this girl and I asked her to move in with me. The next six months were awesome. We shared the coolest relationship. I was starting to feel a bit better.

But after a while I started being mean to Gillian. I feel sorry now because I know how much Mel's constant calls hurt her and, because what Mel was doing to me really messed up my mind, I took it out on Gillian, to my regret. To be honest, I still had feelings for Mel.

As my relationship with Gillian became more serious, I started to shun her. She couldn't understand what was wrong. One time I had some work planned in Orlando and she wanted to come with me. I told her not to bother because I'd be really busy with meetings.

'Can't we just be friends, like we were before?' I said to her.

I wanted my freedom back. I was still discovering myself. Finally, I told her the relationship wasn't working. Looking back, I was very selfish. Gillian had done nothing wrong but I hurt her badly. At that stage of my life I was confused and not ready to settle down. By contrast, with Kate it's so right because I'm now a much more content person and ready to commit to a relationship.

As Claire had predicted, things didn't go as I expected in the States. My encounter with Sonnenberg was fruitless. I was writing and recording but the record company didn't do anything public with me at all; they just kept me in the studios churning out material that I felt no one was going to hear.

Not surprisingly, the panic attacks came back with a vengeance, and I convinced myself that my whole career was over. I had to tell my boss at DAS, Scott McCracken, that I was ill and he sent me to a therapist called Dr Brodie, one of the top shrinks in the States. His diagnosis was gloomy. 'It sounds like your panic attacks could be psychotic,' he said. That was a shock. I'm the most laid-back guy you could meet. But he suggested I spend two weeks in a psychiatric

home in New York. Thank goodness Mum and Dad knew
nothing about it at the time.

It was hell in there and I thought it was all over for me.
But it was worse for my brothers, who had to sit and watch
me suffering in the company of people in straitjackets,
people who would rock back and forwards all day in total
silence, people who were obviously suffering from serious
mental illness. One woman had been tripping on LSD since
1973 and uttered nothing but gobbledegook all day.

I even started praying they wouldn't let me out so that I
couldn't do anything wrong in the outside world. Then
they said they were sending me to another ward and I spent
two weeks there. Deep in my heart I knew it would be a
temporary thing and at least I felt safe. This is probably one
of the most well-known psychiatric institutions in the
world and I'm in here, I thought. I can't believe it! What am
I doing here?

But soon I became really interested in psychology and
before long I was leading the other patients along in our
group therapy sessions. I was really inquisitive and all the
time wanted to learn. I'd ask questions about family
because, unlike me, many of the others had never received
any love from their parents and, like me, had been picked on
at school.

Three people were crying in the session the day I left the
hospital. I didn't feel cured myself and when I got into a taxi
I screamed, 'Let me out, let me out' as I thought the car was
about to implode. My brother Chris took me into Central
Park and we sat down. Whenever I looked up,
hallucinations took over and I could see people falling from

the trees. It must have been a result of all the medication I was taking.

I went back to my doctor and he said, 'To be honest, I've never met somebody like you before. You seem so normal but are obviously completely confused inside.' He referred me to another doctor and then another. Things were getting worse. Every time Mum and Dad rang I told them I was fine. They still thought I was recording.

I became terribly scared of heights and knives. Whenever I booked into a hotel and was staying any higher than the third floor, I'd make a member of staff lock all the windows as I was frightened I might try to jump out in the middle of the night. I'd never order a steak because I knew they'd bring steak knives, so I'd only order dishes like spaghetti. Often I'd be in the middle of a busy restaurant and I'd simply break down and cry. Or I would have a shower and feel I was on the brink of ending it all.

I was completely on my own but I couldn't even think of having a girlfriend. I just didn't know what was going on in my world and couldn't understand why I was being made to suffer like this. Was I being punished for all the things I'd done with girls? That was just one of the crazy thoughts that kept buzzing round inside my head.

I was still all over the place and I just didn't think I was going to get better. My management had set up more writing work for me and persuaded me it would be good for my state of mind if I got out of New York and went to Los Angeles, where the pace of life would be more relaxed. No police sirens day and night and all that sunshine, right?

In Los Angeles I stayed in a beautiful place just off

Sunset Boulevard. I'd already met Rod Stewart and his wife Rachel Hunter at the Gold Cup in Dubai and our get-together was great, so whenever Claire was in LA she would arrange for the four of us to meet for lunch, dinner or sometimes just drinks.

Rod must have been familiar with my success because, when we were invited to a celebrity dinner one evening in Dubai, he asked Claire and me to join him and his family at his table. I couldn't believe it. Compared with a superstar like Rod, I was a virtual nobody. Fortunately, we all hit it off – in fact, Rachel and Claire got on so well that Claire began to manage her, an arrangement which still works now, seven years on – and Rod invited us to join him and Rachel for dinner the following night.

I really like Rod. He once said to me, 'Play the media like they play you. Give them what *you* want but make them think it's what *they* want.' That was such good advice – probably the best I've ever received from someone in the music industry. It all makes sense now. Thanks, Rod.

One night Claire invited us all to go and see a young group she was handling called My Town. They were Irish boys who eventually toured America with Christina Aguilera, but in those days they were just starting out in the States. Rachel's sister, Jackie, who worked as her PA, came along that night and I took a liking to her straight away. I'll always be grateful to Jackie for everything she did for me; without her TLC, my head would never have been straightened out.

After the show I asked her if she fancied going for a drink once we'd said goodbye to everyone, and I suggested a little bar nearby. Jackie was a superb surfer, like so many New

Zealanders, so she was in pretty good shape. Nature quickly took its course and we hit it off big time. Jackie was very loving and caring and we had a wonderful sexual relationship that lasted for quite a while. Sadly, as we grew closer over the coming months, Rod and Rachel were drifting apart. It was so very sad seeing such a great couple falling out of love. But we all had some good times together.

Eventually, as our relationship progressed, I felt I had to tell Jackie what was wrong with me and warn her that I might not get any better. To my amazement, she brushed aside my fears and told me, 'Well, Rod's had a similar thing – especially since the break-up with Rachel – and he's seeing a specialist who's really good. She's really helping him.'

I made an appointment to see the therapist, who straight away said I should stop taking my medication and concentrate instead on talking to her so that we could get to the bottom of what was bugging me.

Over the next few months we worked hard together and it became more and more clear to both of us that everything that was tormenting me stemmed from the mental trauma I had undergone during the years in Australia. She helped me to see that I actually hated my work and way of life, and that together they were destroying me. I felt constantly forced into situations where I wasn't comfortable. I'd had all those number ones but I had no money. I wasn't broke but I should have been a rich young man.

What particularly tormented me was the idea that all my talent had been thrown away by people who cared more about themselves than me. Another important thing that my therapist pointed out was that for the past few years I hadn't had a base to give me a sense of security. All that time I'd been living out of suitcases.

After starting to see my therapist I began to feel better straight away, and, although the panic attacks still happened every day, they became less frequent.

'Don't see this as a breakdown, Peter,' she told me. 'See it as a breakthrough.' This is great advice that I frequently pass on to Kate.

My sessions with the therapist went on for about a year. I talked to her about things I'd never spoken about before and bawled my eyes out. I closed a chapter in my life. Now I started to pray and promise never to take what I have for granted again. I just wanted to wake up and think, Wow, what a beautiful day! In time I closed a painful chapter in my life. I was no longer lost in my own world.

And thank goodness Jackie and Rachel were there to put the laughter back into my life. One night after I had been in the studio all day, I got back to my hotel to find a message waiting for me on the answering machine in my room. 'Hi, Peter, this is Rachel,' said a very sexy voice. 'I'm here with my lovely sister. We're just about to get into the hot tub and we're wondering if you'd like to come and join us. Call me back within an hour.'

The message was timed at nine in the evening, but by then it was almost two in the morning. I was gutted. What an experience that would have been!

CHAPTER EIGHT

RESPECT YOURSELF

ALTHOUGH MY PROFESSIONAL arrangement with Claire had ended, I still met her from time to time when she came to the States to see Rachel. 'You should've stayed with me!' she'd tell me. And you know what, she was right. Being axed by Mushroom got me more bad press, as happens when any British label drops you. People I thought had been my friends turned on me. I was a 'pop flop' all over again. I couldn't take any more, so I took the easy way out. I just walked away from it all and turned my back on the life I had dreamed about but which had been nothing more than one long nightmare.

But I had launched a last-ditch attempt to make it in the States after meeting Lou Pearlman in January 2000. Three years earlier Lou and his colleague Johnny had contacted Claire for tips on breaking his new band, the Backstreet Boys, in Britain. I was presenting a *Smash Hits* tour in association with the magazine at the time and he couldn't believe the fan base I'd developed.

I learned that Lou was staying at Le Park Suites. As I was staying in the same hotel, I knocked on his suite door. What greeted me was, to put it politely, the strangest sight I've ever seen. There was Lou, a 20-stone man, standing in his boxers! We looked at each other and laughed. He reached over and gave me a very big and sincere hug – although obviously he put some clothes on first! We spoke for over an hour.

'I'll break you in America,' he promised. 'Coke, Pepsi... I'll introduce you to all the right people.'

So I signed a deal with Lou. I even flew my parents out to see me sign the contracts; that's how much I was convinced things would work out this time round. To this day I still regard Lou Pearlman as one of the most polite and generous men in the business. Shortly after I signed a deal, I bumped into Kevin Richardson of the Backstreet Boys at a cinema in LA.

He said, 'Why don't you hook up a meeting with me and AJ McLean? Sign to our label and we'll tour the States together.' AJ was also a member of the Backstreet Boys.

But I told them it was too late. I really kick myself now for not taking them up on their offer. Each time at my own expense, I flew to Orlando for several meetings with Lou, who insisted that I'd only make it if I got my abs back. I thought I'd grown out of all that! I felt a pressure to be in shape whenever we had meetings. He did, however, introduce me to representatives from Coke and Pepsi.

Within six months of signing to Lou, I realised I was heading down a dead-end road. I wanted to show I had some faith in him, but I think a year and a half of loyalty to someone who hasn't brought you many results is fair. Then, in September 2001, the 9/11 disaster happened and we agreed to part.

Despite everything, I still have a great respect for Lou. He made me believe I could make it again. I started to believe in myself, but I was no longer so desperate to be a star. And that helped. Instead of looking at my bad experience as a negative, I started to see it as a positive. I felt I was in control of my life for the first time. I may not have had much money, but at least I wasn't at the beck and call of people any more. I even started accepting what my critics were saying about me. And after a few months I started thinking, You know what? I'm stronger, I'm stronger, I'm stronger, I'm stronger. But even today I still take the odd bit of medication because I'm scared of a relapse.

When I was dropped by Mushroom in 2000, it wasn't the end of the world for me. In a way, deep inside I wanted them to let me go, because I had been stalling for almost three years about releasing new songs. By the time I had got over my lack of confidence in myself and my music, the market had changed a bit. We had the family business in Australia, in which I had invested some of my earnings from music, so I decided I would go back there and give Mum and Dad a break from running it. I eased off on the training and started to live my life from where I left off at 17. I was so happy. I had felt so trapped in the music business and now I was free.

For a while I ran the resort with one of my brothers, and my parents took it easy. It was hard work for me but relaxing in a way. I was a receptionist, one of the chefs and one of the cleaners, a maitre d' and a bartender for the resort. But it was therapy for me. I was so busy. I was learning new things and loving it.

I returned to my wild ways with women, although this time I experienced a guilt I'd never felt before. Very quickly I lost respect for myself. Now I didn't get the same pleasure and enjoyment from those conquests. I was better than that and those girls were better than that.

One day I got a phone call from my cousin Alexi in London, who said he'd met a guy called Ron Winters, who worked for RMG, the Ritz Music Group. My cousin worked in a shop and Winters came in to buy something and they got talking about music. Alexi mentioned me and Winters said he was dying to get hold of me. He was supposed to have lots of artists on his label and apparently thought I could make it big again. No harm in seeing what it's all about, I thought. I checked with Claire, but she didn't know much about Ron and suggested I give him a call to sound him out.

'You need to get over here quick because we're going to make you a huge star again,' Ron told me. 'Now's the right time for you. You've been gone long enough.'

'I don't know if I really want to do this any more, Ron,' I protested. 'I'm starting to find myself now and I'm really happy.'

In the end, things between me and Ron didn't work out.

While I was in England I met up with Claire again and she commiserated with me that my attempt to do business with Winters hadn't worked out, especially as it had cost me a lot of money. I couldn't decide where to go next, since all my investments were in Australia and if I was to stay on in

England I'd have to get money wired to me every week or so. I didn't fancy the idea of losing money every time because of the exchange rate, which at the time was three Australian dollars to the pound.

So then I thought of Cyprus and my roots. The family had an apartment there and I decided I would fly out and lie low for a while. When I got there, it only took me a day or two to get the property bug. Land was so cheap and the life so good there that I just had to buy a place of my own. But I wasn't content to buy a house, I wanted a big plot of land so I could build my own place to my design and my taste. Suddenly the crazy world of music seemed such a long way away, and I knew I was finding myself at last.

But as I was buying the land another opportunity came my way, and I jumped at it. I bought a gym and went into partnership with my brother Michael. Downstairs was a beauty salon and my sister Debbie was just the right person to run that part of the business. Soon we were doing really well and having a relaxing time too. I was my own boss, taking orders from no one, and life was cool. For once I was training others rather than putting myself through it, and I loved every moment of it. Before we knew it, Mikey, Debbie and I were transforming people's lives.

It was brilliant. People would come over to the gym to hang out with us. Everyone felt so comfortable at our gym. We packed it out. It was one of the busiest gyms because everyone looked at it as a night out. I used to teach classes downstairs. I had nothing to lose and nothing to gain. Financially I had all my money tied up in investments. No cash whatsoever. I had property with Dad in Australia, I had just bought a massive plot of land in Cyprus and I co-owned a gym, so I knew that I would never go hungry, but I was loving the fact that I was earning next to nothing. For once in my life 50 pence meant something! My lifestyle was simple and I loved it. I could have got a loan against my investments but I never did. I never ever took for granted the fact that I could have still lived that lifestyle even when things were quiet.

I'd finally found myself and was happy with my life. For the first time ever I was at peace with myself.

CHAPTER NINE
RISKING IT ALL

DOCTORS WOULD CALL what I had been through a breakdown. But, like my therapist, I call my experience a breakthrough, because it was as if I had died and been reborn. It completely changed my life.

It happened the day I decided to stop being obsessed with the gym. It was the day I decided I'd rather be happy and have nothing than have everything and be unhappy. It was the day I decided I'd been taking the music industry too seriously. I needed to look at the bigger picture of my life rather than let music be the only thing in focus. It was the day my love towards my mum, dad, brothers and sister grew and I started realising that a lot of the people that were around me were just hanging on. They weren't real friends. It was the time I knew I didn't want to sleep around any more. Everything changed.

But the experience was hell. It was as if all the bad things in my life were being flashed in front of me for one last time, just to teach me a lesson. It's a horrible experience which you never think you're going to survive. I liken it to when you're flying and you hit the clouds and turbulence. After a bumpy ride you suddenly hit clear blue sky again. The problems are beneath you and you feel so free. Most people live their lives in the turbulent clouds and I felt like I was in one that I just couldn't get out of. And then one day I saw light and I was finally in that clear blue sky that never dies. In fact, shortly after this I wrote a song called 'Broken Man' with a brilliant pianist, Aristos Moskiovakis, which uses those exact words.

But I didn't want to break all my links with the past. One day in LA I rang my former manager in London and said, 'Claire, I've been going through a really bad experience emotionally but I'm getting through it now. If you think there's anything in England for me, do you want to redo a management deal?'

'Pete, you know you hurt me last time. I put everything into breaking you.'

'Yeah, I know, but there were reasons I can't explain. I had to leave. I can't explain it to you. Not yet!'

'You know I'll manage you if anything comes up, Pete. I always keep an eye open for opportunities for you.'

'I'm not going to hold my breath, but, if you think there is anything for me, just let me know. I'm going to move to Cyprus and start something new, but you can always get hold of me any time.'

I felt so happy and positive, because Claire is the one person in the business I'd trust with my life and I knew she was one of the best managers around.

65

PETER ANDRE

MYSTERIOUS GIRL

PETER ANDRE

Surrounded by my 'Mysterious Girl' memorabilia (love those big pants!). It took three releases and three chart placings to get to number one. It finally hit the top spot when it was re-released after I came out of the jungle.

Messing around on our first holiday together in Cyprus.

ove: Katie and I celebrating my 32nd birthday at Planet Hollywood in Orlando.

low: In our home recording studio. Katie was eight months pregnant with Junior when
s picture was taken.

Things may have looked steamy when Katie joined in with shooting the video for 'The Right Way' but it was freezing at Camber Sands

Above: A slightly warmer location was found for shooting the rest of 'The Right Way'.

Below: Hello sailor! On board the love boat in the USA.

Above: Myself, Katie and our parents on board the Caribbean cruise, which didn't go quite as well as I had hoped.

Inset: With my best friend George Nicolaou on board the cruise.

Below: Celebrating my mum and dad's 50th wedding anniversary. *From left to right*: My brothers Danny and Mike, me, Katie, my sister Debbie, my niece Thea, my sister-in-law Pam and my brothers Andrew and Chris.

...rs I have known and loved. My Porsche 911 convertible (above) and the sleek ...ercedes S Class.

Now it's all about us.

An offer came up to do *Celebrity Big Brother* and I turned it down. Thanks, but no thanks. What was I going to do on *Celebrity Big Brother*? Sit in a room all day and let people watch me having panic attacks?

This was followed by an offer to do *Celebrity Boxing*. That didn't tempt me either. The third offer was for an eight-week series called *The Club*. I didn't want to do that, but I was concerned that, if I kept on turning down every offer, no one would want to put work my way. So I didn't say no and I didn't say yes. The money would have been nice, but I wasn't sure I wanted the aggravation of leaving Cyprus for that length of time. In the end the decision was made for me. I kept hoping the TV company would decide I wasn't suitable for the show – and they did. Thank God for that!

Finally, Claire rang me with an offer to appear in a new series of *I'm A Celebrity Get Me Out Of Here!* I hadn't heard of it before and I was intrigued by the title, so I asked what it was all about.

'Well, it's like a *Survivor* challenge,' Claire said.

'I'll do it,' I said straight off.

'Are you sure?'

'I'll do it.'

'Don't you want to know the full details about the show?'

'No. I'll do it.'

'Don't you even want to see videos of the last series?'

'No.'

Something was telling me that this was meant to be. Never in my wildest dreams did I imagine that *I'm A Celebrity...* was about to change my whole life all over again by introducing me to the most amazing woman I'd ever met

– or could ever wish to meet. She was the woman I was about to fall in love with. Katie Price, aka Jordan.

After I said I'd do the show, ITV wanted to meet me to make sure I'd be suitable. Here we go again, I thought. I'm gonna fly myself over and they're going to stand me up. But they didn't and we got on very well. They asked me to pose for a photo shoot with all the jungle paraphernalia. I hadn't done work like this in years and suddenly I felt self-conscious about my body. Then the doubts really started to set in. Oh my God, have I done the right thing? What if I have a panic attack in the jungle live on TV? But then I told myself, No, I'm strong now.

I'd always loved shows like *Survivor* and I reminded myself that, even if it turned out to be harder than I expected, I'd only be in the jungle for two weeks. I might even be evicted after a week, and what's a week of hardship? It would be the experience of a lifetime, I could raise money for charity, plus I'd be getting paid for it too. But what made it all happen? What led me to meet Katie? What took me from going there thinking, I just want to get through the two weeks, to meeting my wife and not wanting to leave because I didn't want to be away from her for a minute.

Because I'd been moving round the world and then been in self-imposed hibernation for so long, I was really out of touch with what had been going on in Britain. For a start, I'd never heard of a Page Three girl called Jordan. I'd never seen her in any papers or magazines. Nor had I heard of Jennie Bond, Lord Brocket, Diane Modahl or Mike Read. The only one of the celebrities I'd heard of was John Lydon, aka Johnny Rotten, because my brothers were mad on the Sex

Pistols when we were kids. I was a bit apprehensive about meeting him because everyone kept winding me up and telling me he'd probably spend his time trying to pick a fight with me.

Not that I was really worried. 'I bet you any money he'll be a barking dog,' I said. 'I bet he's a nice bloke who just acts up for the cameras.' And, as it turned out, Johnny Rotten and I used to sit up late at night when everyone else was asleep and talk. We bonded because of cigarettes.

On the day I left London for the jungle my management team showed me a photo of Jordan, so I'd recognise her when we met, and Claire had some memorable advice for me: 'Pete, stay away from her and you will get through.' And her people said the same thing to her about me: 'Stay away from him or you'll get screwed.'

It's a good job we didn't listen. I love Claire and she's been so good for me, but I have to say that on this occasion the advice was wrong, even though it was given with the best of intentions. Even while I was in the jungle, Claire warned my parents, 'If he goes on with this romance it's going to wreck his chances of restarting his career. She's known for leading guys on then dumping them.' Amy, Katie's mum, thought the same about me in terms of Katie's career. The comments Claire made about Katie were based on what she had read in the press, before she actually met her and got to know her.

I first met Katie the day before we all went into the jungle. I couldn't believe that she was the same girl I'd seen in the photo. She looked harmless and I wanted to like her personality straight away. She was very pretty. I didn't study her body, as she was fully clothed, but I could see she wasn't at all overweight. I have to be totally honest and say that all I remembered later were her eyes and her braided hair. She looked like Bo Derek from the film *10*. Suddenly I felt at ease. She's not going to be a problem, I decided. But at the time I had no intentions whatsoever. I didn't even want to allow myself to think anything like that.

Katie shook my hand with a really strong grip and said, 'All right?' I never called her Jordan, even on that first day.

The truth is, I saw straight through her from day one. Beneath the barriers and the brash act, deep down inside she was a sweet girl who wanted to be loved by somebody. I knew later I could be the one guy to tame the lioness. Not because I'm a hero, but because I knew that all she needed was security. The minute she got it, the barriers started coming down.

I noticed she wasn't happy with herself; she had no make-up on and she wouldn't look me in the eye. It wasn't because she liked me, it was because she hated the fact that someone would look at her in that bare way. The next thing I noticed were her breasts. She'd obviously got them as big as she could so that attention would be taken away from everywhere else and focused on something that she was happy with. It was not really her, but she had control over it.

I started getting these flashbacks and thinking, That's what I used to do. I used to go out with the shirt open as far down as possible because it took attention away from my face. I hated my face and I hated my nose. I hated so many things about me that I wanted people to focus on my chest. Had I met my match? It was too bizarre. It was as if she was me in a female body – except she was far more attractive than I ever was!

Within two hours of talking to her, I told her that it was all an act on her part. She was really fiery and said, 'What you talking about?'

'I can see straight through you,' I replied.

By now she was getting really agitated and I knew that I had her exactly where I wanted her.

At that point I wasn't sure how I felt about Katie. But I found her fascinating. Whatever it was, I couldn't tear myself away from her. I knew that if I started coming on to someone in the show I'd be looked on as a sleazy guy. My brother Michael gave me two pieces of advice. 'Whatever you do, Pete, don't flirt,' he said, 'and don't sing on camera, because, however you sing, you'll look like an idiot.' And he was right!

I'm a very determined person, so, for me to fall for her without actually wanting to, it must have been love. Katie tells me she was attracted to me before we started talking. She says she felt it the second she saw me. Before entering the jungle she'd had someone read her cards and they told her the person she'd marry would be of Mediterranean origin, wearing a suit, would have dark hair and that she would meet him in an exotic location. Believe it or not, I was wearing a suit that night as I'd been told to treat it like a business meeting. She has told me time and time again that the second I walked in she felt a nervousness she'd never felt before.

We all sat down at a table and she started speaking really loudly, making it very clear that she wanted to be heard by everyone.

'Things aren't working between me and Scott. I've come to the jungle to clear my mind. I know he's not right for me. He knows it's over.'

Yes! I said to myself straight away. If I'd known that she was genuinely in love with someone, being the person that I now am, I may as well have cut my throat rather than try to come on to her.

I'd never gone for a girl with green eyes and blonde hair before. I'd been with girls with green eyes and dark skin, but I'd only ever been out with one blonde in my life and that was Melanie Cooper when I was sweet 17. But here I was finding myself swept along by feelings I had never known before.

My feelings grew stronger the following day when we were preparing ourselves for the 'bush trials'. We were all driven a few miles into the jungle to start to get used to our new surroundings, the heat, the bugs and the demands that were going to be placed on us, both physical and mental. I was lucky enough to be in the back of one of the cars with Katie, but we hardly spoke.

As we took part in those preliminary bush trials, I got a distinct taste of what the next two weeks were going to be like. There was a contest to see who could hog the cameras and who could be the loudest – won easily by Brocket, Razor Ruddock, Katie and Kerry McFadden. They all wanted to show what they could do, so with Mike Read, Diane Modahl and Jennie Bond I just hung back and let them get on with it. I was convinced I would be the first one to be voted out, and told Diane so. The bookies had been offering very short odds on me lasting more than a day or two.

Standing in the shadows enabled me to watch Katie more closely. I couldn't help being attracted to her but there's no denying that her loud, over-the-top antics were putting me off a little. And I really didn't like the way the four main contenders were trying to outdo one another. I reckoned that if we were all to come through this we had to be more of a team.

Was it my own insecurity after the experiences I had gone through that was making me wary of getting too close to Katie? Maybe it was. Somehow I didn't want to take the gamble of being hurt. I wanted to try to survive two weeks, raise the money for my charity, make a little for myself, maybe do something small with my musical career for a while and then go back and retreat into the comfortable lifestyle I had built up in Cyprus.

As time went on that day I got the distinct impression that Katie was glancing my way now and again, as if she was looking for a response from me. I wasn't completely sure. I thought maybe I was just flattering myself that she would look at me that way. If she was looking, perhaps it wasn't mutual attraction but because she wanted attention. She certainly managed to grab it from the camera.

When Bushtucker Bill said we should hold some giant grubs for one of the trials, most of us pulled faces. Not Katie – she was the first to get them in her hands, quickly followed by Razor, Brocket and Kerry. Then Bill told us the grubs were edible and, quick as a flash, Katie had one in her mouth. God, you're brave, I thought. But then I noticed the way she was sucking on the grub, trying to make it look horny.

It left me cold. Yet all the while, as Katie was playing up to the cameras, I knew she was also sneaking little sideways glances at me to see what my reaction was. She acted all brash and harsh, but when no one was talking to her she'd go into this quiet state and she'd be thinking.

When Bill told me to pick up a witchety grub everyone was quiet except Katie. 'Oh, don't be stupid, just put it in your mouth,' she taunted. That was her way of trying to communicate with me. God, I thought, you're making it a bit blatant that you just want to have a conversation. She kept on at me and I'd notice little things that she'd say and do that were quite predictable.

I really didn't know what to make of it. Was she setting me up for a major fall? Was she going to chew me up and spit me out like that giant grub she'd had between her lips? I was confused, but in a strange way I was excited too. A delicious sense of anticipation was mounting by the minute.

On the drive back to the hotel, Katie and I again sat in the back seat together, with Jennie Bond up front with the driver. The banter was non-stop.

'I bet you're one of these really sleazy guys,' Katie said to me. 'Did you have a shower this morning? Have you brushed your teeth today? 'Cos you smell a bit funny!'

'It's funny you should say that about teeth,' I hit back. 'Are yours fake?'

'Yes, I've had them capped.'

'You know they're turning black on the tops, don't you?'

'Oh get lost, they're not.'

I could see I was starting to get to her.

'With your hair like that, you do know what the spiders

will do?' I said. 'They'll nest in the place that doesn't move. You'll have to shake them out in the morning.'

But she didn't give up the fight easily. After a minute or two of silence, she sprung this one on me: 'I bet you've got black satin sheets on your bed at home.'

'Get lost!'

'I bet you have.'

'No, I haven't. But seven or eight years ago I did.'

'Oh, you're such a sleazebag! Get away from me!'

So I went back to her teeth again. 'You are bringing floss in the jungle, aren't you? You've got to do something about those teeth of yours.'

We were giving each other so much grief that eventually Jennie turned round and looked at the two of us, smiling knowingly.

'Jennie, for Katie to give me this much shit,' I said, 'she must like me a little bit. Just a little bit.'

That made Katie furious. 'Oh, don't flatter yourself,' she said.

'Come on, Katie,' I teased her. 'You're giving me all this grief and I've said nothing to you. That must mean you like me.'

Jennie smiled again and said in a tone of mock surprise, 'Oh my God, the chemistry's there already between you two.'

But Katie was adamant. 'What are you talking about, Jennie? Chemistry between us? Oh my God, are you joking? Please tell me you are.'

I tried again. 'Aw, come on. Admit it. You do like me a little.' And then Katie laughed and I knew that was it. There was something there.

But I had to defend myself, stop myself falling into this trap. So I tried to keep it light-hearted. 'You can admit you like me, Katie. Jennie's not going to tell anyone.'

When we got to the hotel we got out of the car and Katie turned to me to say goodbye. Wanting to be a gentleman, I offered her my hand and as she shook it she did the most amazing thing. She squeezed my hand, then rubbed her thumb across the top of it. A shock ran through me and I felt like I was a little boy again with my first girlfriend. Even writing about it now, I get goosebumps just thinking about what that subtle message was telling me.

Katie and the other girls went to their rooms to shower and get ready for an early night because we had to be up at three the next morning. Being daft blokes, Razor, Brocket, Mike Read, me and the others headed for the bar.

I turned to my big brother Andrew and said, 'Mate, I'm not interested in this at all.'

'Can't say I blame you,' he said. 'Tell you what, where's Jordan? I'd like to meet her.'

I had no idea where she was, but Andrew said I should call her room and ask her to come down for a drink.

'No way, man. I'm not calling her room. Do you think I'm stupid?'

'Come on, brother. Call her.'

Then the others in the bar joined in. 'Yeah, Pete, call Katie, call Katie.'

Eventually I plucked up courage to ring her. Her mother, Amy, answered the phone and I could tell from her tone that she didn't much like me. Later she admitted as much to me, though we're great friends now.

I said, 'Listen, my brother's here, everyone's downstairs, and we're all just wondering if Katie wants to come down for a quick drink? That's all.'

Amy turned away from the phone and said, 'It's Peter. He wants to know if you fancy a drink.' In the background I heard Katie's brusque reply: 'Tell him I'm knackered.'

What an idiot I felt hanging on that phone. It was real teenage stuff. I wondered if maybe I had totally misread the signs earlier on, that the romance was just a figment of my imagination. Katie didn't come down for a drink and all I could do was ask myself why I'd even bothered inviting her. I was convinced her refusal was her way of making clear she just wasn't interested in me.

I stayed down in the bar for a drink with the others and got talking to one of the security guards from the hotel. She was called Angie and I had taken a liking to her as she was from the Gold Coast too, so we knew a lot of the same places. She had once been a dancer and was very attractive.

Shortly after 3am, as it was just starting to get light, we all gathered in the hotel lobby. Now I felt really nervous. More than anything, I wasn't sure quite how I'd survive without coffee! A huge breakfast had arrived at my room that morning, but I couldn't eat anything. All I did was drink coffee. I must have had five cups in the hour before we all met up downstairs. Amusingly, the only other thing I couldn't live without was some hair wax. I was really concerned my hair would go wiry and turn Afro-style in the heat. Claire helped me wrap some wax in cling film and I stuffed it down my pants, just below my bum. Typical! While everyone else was smuggling essentials like salt and pepper, my main worry was my hair.

Kate came down for breakfast with Amy and her son Harvey. I took to him straight away – he's a gorgeous little fella – but there was no spark between her and me at that moment in time.

This is not going to happen, I thought. And that was good, because I didn't really want it to. But you know how it is; no sooner had that thought gone through my mind than I was telling myself the exact opposite. She must like me a little bit. Maybe she's just better at the game than I am.

The production crew did a quick head count to make sure we were all present and ready to move out. As we hung around in the lobby, waiting for our transport, I spotted Angie and found myself saying, 'When I come back would you like to meet and have a coffee?' She said she'd love to.

Suddenly, as we prepared to get into our limos, Kerry blurted out, 'Oh look, there's Angie, Peter! There's Angie! Have you said goodbye?' I admitted I hadn't, so she got out of the car and said bossily, 'You must say goodbye to the girl.'

Then Katie joined in, with undisguised sarcasm, 'Yeah, go and say bye to your Angie!' And that was the first time I saw Katie's cute face turn green.

She's jealous, I thought. Katie's jealous. Jordan is jealous of me!

She said it again. 'Yeah, go, go. Go and see Angie! See if you can have a coffee with her when you get back.'

How the hell did she know about that? Who'd been blabbing? I knew at once it must have been Kerry. But I thought I'd see how far I could push my luck with Katie, now that I knew she did have some kind of feeling for me, so

I nipped out of the car, strolled over to Angie and gave her a peck on the cheek to say goodbye.

When I got back in the car and sat next to Katie again, I could see her ego had been ever so slightly deflated. So I said, 'Oh dear, what's wrong? Isn't everyone going, "Ooh, Jordan, Jordan?" Don't you like it? Are you mad 'cos everyone's saying, "Angie, Angie"?'

Katie was getting pretty agitated now. It didn't help when everyone else in the limo just started laughing. And kept on laughing all the way to the helipad. A crowd of photographers were waiting by the helicopter and you can guess who pushed their way right to the front – Razor, Brocket, Kerry and, naturally, Katie.

Up until then I'd been more than happy to keep out of the way. But suddenly I had an overwhelming urge to stand as close as I could to Katie. It was almost as if a magnetic force was drawing us together.

I struck lucky and managed to sit next to her in the helicopter too. The 90-minute flight to the jungle landing area was a magical one that I still relive over and over in my mind. The sky was a mixture of a thousand colours as dawn broke over to our right and the early morning washed over the mountains below us.

There was an unmistakably intense chemistry between the two of us. Katie's bare leg, clad in her bush shorts, was pressing firmly against mine throughout the flight. As I pushed harder against her, she pushed back. All the time I had to fight the urge to put my hand on her thigh and, funnily enough, she told me months later that the very same idea had been going through her mind. Without a doubt, that flight was the most romantic experience of my life. We didn't do anything except press our legs together – we didn't even say a word – but it was one of those moments that make a deep impression on you and which you never forget. You know what love is when you don't have to speak. It's when the little things simplify even the most complicated situations.

Without a shadow of doubt, I was falling in love.

To this day people believe that our relationship was just a stunt, scripted for the programme. They think the producers were clever enough to choose Peter Andre and Katie Price, from all the people in showbiz around the world, to create an artificial romance. But the truth, as everyone knows now, is very simple: we fell in love. Nobody told us to, we just did.

CHAPTER TEN
JUNGLE OF LOVE

LANDING WAS SCARY because we had to fly very close to the mountains and suddenly drop down into a small clearing among the trees. I thought we were going to crash and when we got out of the helicopter my heart was really thumping. But maybe that was because throughout the flight I had been mentally making love to Katie!

The producers had told us we'd have a bit of a walk, but they didn't tell us how far it would be or how long it would take. We were all shattered after the first hour and we were still only a third of the way there.

From the start Katie had gone straight over to join Razor, Alex, Kerry and Brocket, so I stayed back with Johnny, Mike, Diane and Jennie. They were all being loud, playing up to the cameras and flirting with one another. Once again I started to have doubts about whether there really was anything between Katie and I. Maybe it had all been just a weird fantasy. Whatever was happening, it was certainly confusing!

The cameras were on us all the way as we followed arrows through the trees and the undergrowth, but the camera crews weren't allowed to talk to us or offer us any help or advice. When the show went out on TV our trek had been edited down to a couple of minutes that didn't give a true picture of how tough it was.

We went up hill and down dale, and the further we went the hotter and more humid it became. The first sight of camp was such a relief, although once we'd had a good look round we were all amazed at how basic it was. But that didn't stop some of the selfish bastards from running straight to the best beds and saying, 'I'll have this one, you find your own.'

What we didn't know was that there were ten of us but only seven beds. There was a hammock as well but still two beds had to be built from scratch. We'd been shown the day before how to put a bed together and I wasn't very good at it, so stupidly I volunteered to have the hammock. It was the worst choice I could have made. As I was to find out to my cost, you only had to turn over too quickly in your sleep and you'd be dumped on your arse on the floor.

Once the sleeping arrangements had been sorted out we moved on to the food. We'd found our supply of rice, beans and cooking oil and measured it out. It had to last three days and we couldn't believe how little there was. We were sure we were all going to starve because our ration of rice was just one and a half tablespoons a day each. The whole pile of rice would barely make a decent meal for two, but we had to share it out between ten of us over three days.

This can't be right, I thought. But then, unlike any of the

others, I'd never seen the show before on TV and didn't know what to expect. Add to that confusion my roller-coaster emotions with Katie and you'll understand that I was in a bit of a state at the end of that very tiring first day. Everyone agreed that after what we'd been through it was most definitely time for bed, so I headed off for my hammock. As soon as my head touched the pillow, I was asleep. And no sooner had I fallen asleep than I dropped off again, this time literally. Bang! I fell straight out of the hammock. It was one hell of a shock. I didn't know where I was or what I was doing. I didn't really even know who I was. I just knew I had a pretty sore body where I'd landed on the hard ground.

Undaunted, I climbed back into the hammock – and promptly fell straight out of the other side. That happened to me for the next four nights, almost on the hour, and I was getting barely two hours' sleep a night because of my painful tumbles. Jennie, God bless her, asked every day if I wanted her bed. So did a couple of the others, but I didn't have the heart to say yes. After all, I thought, I'm only here for two weeks, so losing sleep won't kill me.

But my night-time starvation had a greater effect than I could have imagined, and those first two or three days were very disorientating. I was in a daze and not really in touch with what was going on. I shrank into my shell and all I could hear all the time were the loud ones sitting round the campfire singing.

Katie says she kept trying to catch my eye all the time, hoping I'd be looking at her, but in all honesty I never noticed. At night I'd lie in that bloody awful hammock and think, I wish she'd come over and talk to me. Why is she sitting on Razor's lap, why is she sitting next to Brocket, when she won't even come near me?

I wasn't jealous of them. No way! But I did keep asking myself, Am I that ugly or what? Or does she really hate me? Or does she like me that much that she has to avoid me? I don't get it.

Although I was determined to remain in the background, I did one very vain thing on our first day. I was hot and I really wanted to take my shirt off, but I knew if I stood there bare-chested in front of all of them they'd just think I was trying to show off my body. Though I say it myself, my six pack and my biceps and shoulders were in great shape, which is hardly surprising since I owned a gym and had been training hard for the previous few weeks. I'd been warned that there would be a man-eater on the show who would probably try to embarrass me in front of the nation, so I worked hard to look good as that was the only weapon I had.

It got hotter and hotter and I knew that shirt just had to come off. I wanted Katie to see that I was all man – guys are like that. Why else do you think we spend hours sweating it out in the gym? But I was shy. Little Pete just couldn't pluck up courage to show off in front of Big Katie. Oh my God! I'm acting like a teenager again! I realised.

So I got up and walked away from everyone to a quiet spot where I could take my top off and splash some cool water over myself in that 30-degrees-plus heat. Cleverly I made sure that the only person who could see me strip was Katie. I know it's vain, and I know it makes me sound stupid, but I was desperate for her attention. I had to know whether the banter with Razor and the flirting with Brocket meant anything, or whether there might just be a chance that Katie was as interested in me as I was in her.

We have a laugh together about it now. She'll say, 'Pete, do you know how stupid you looked taking your top off like that?' And I'll say, 'Well, you didn't have to look if you didn't want to.'

But she did. Out of the corner of my eye, I could see her nudging Kerry, but fortunately Kerry's line of vision was blocked by a bush and she couldn't see what Katie was making a fuss about.

After a couple of minutes I put my T-shirt back on and sauntered casually back to the others as if nothing had happened. I knew I was being really stupid, and told myself I was a dickhead. The girls were giggling, but I didn't know if it was at me. I felt certain Katie must have been at least a little impressed. How sad was I?

She soon shot me down. 'You know, Pete, you should work on your lower abs, they're not that good. You haven't been training for a while, have you?'

Now I felt a right idiot. I said, 'Get stuffed! Have you seen how flat your arse is?'

And that was it. War was declared. We started picking each other to pieces. Diane Modahl was very sweet and tried to make me feel good by lying that Katie had actually been saying earlier how good I looked. But Katie wasn't having that.

'No I bloody didn't,' she jumped in. 'I was telling you how much he needs to work out.'

That was the moment when I knew she really liked me. She could say what she liked about me, but she still had that look in her eye that told me she didn't mean a word of it. Once again her reaction had been too predictable. In a strange way her hurtful words were almost terms of endearment. It was a similar situation when she later started teasing me about having an acorn. I knew she had so many insecurities. When the cameras weren't rolling she would whisper the most beautiful words and I genuinely believed her.

The beans they gave us to eat had to be soaked in water for 24 hours before being cooked, to soften them up. We were too hungry to wait and decided to eat them raw. They were like rabbit pellets! I refused to eat them. Not only did I know they would upset my stomach, but just the thought of it was making me feel sick. So all I had was my one and a half tablespoons of rice. By mid-afternoon I was in a terrible state. But I couldn't believe Katie: she had eaten her beans and rice, drunk loads of water and then gone to sleep.

Me, I was starving. That whole day I ate barely a tenth of what a normal person would eat for breakfast. The worse I felt, the more my feelings for Katie began to play on my mind. I reckon it's all an act! I finally convinced myself. She's just acting like this in front of the camera. Either that or she's a damn good player! She's playing me about.

On day two I decided I had to force the issue, try to get to the truth, before I drove myself crazy. Katie and I were crouching on our haunches, cleaning some pots, when I turned round to her and said quietly, 'I like you, Katie. I really like you,' and she whispered back, 'I really like you too.'

I couldn't believe my ears. My heart started thumping and I suddenly had butterflies in my stomach. We went back to the camp and I had to collect my thoughts pretty quickly. I said to Katie, 'I'm glad we talked. I'm just going to lie down for a while. I'll see you a bit later on.'

'OK,' she said. 'Whatever.'

It seemed a very sad goodbye after the closeness we'd both expressed just a minute or two earlier.

'Why are you so mean to me?' I asked her.

She just went, 'Um...'

'You said you liked me, and you're nice to me when we're alone, but once the others are around all you want to do is put me down.'

She looked at me as if I was imagining it, and maybe I was. That's what hunger can do to you.

The next day we had just beans and rice again, but then Razor and Katie won the bush trial and won ten stars, earning us a so-called feast. It was minimal food, but anything was better than just rice and beans!

When Katie came back from her trial and told us the good news about the ten stars, we all congratulated her. But once again she treated me as if I wasn't there. So again I thought, Either she really likes me or she absolutely detests me. I can't figure it out.

With her, I was in – out – in – out – in – out. This was supposed to be a game and millions were watching, but it was starting to drive me insane. I was so hungry, I remember thinking, I want to eat, and I want her... Maybe I just want to eat her.

Those first few days in the jungle were very weird. Our

medic, Doctor Bob, warned us we would all feel confused at first as we tried to adjust to our new surroundings. On about the fourth day, he said, the hunger will kick in and people will start to become agitated. And constipated! He was right. By the time we left the jungle we had lost about half a stone – with the exception of Katie, who was eating everything she could lay her hands on, from beans to bugs. She actually put on half a stone, the only person who's ever done that on the show.

It was impossible to keep track of time. After a while I worked out that we were going to sleep about eight o'clock. I knew that in summer in Australia it got dark about 7.30 in January, and that was when they were bringing us our food. And we were waking up just before daybreak, which must have been about four in the morning. The hardest thing for me in the jungle was not the heat, the flies, the lack of food, the discomfort or the spiders. It was the fact that I couldn't have my morning cup of coffee. I rely on caffeine to jolt me into action when I wake up, and without it I was so lethargic.

Despite all the hardship, a real sense of love was developing in the camp. And there were some beautiful moments between Katie and I. On the fourth day I started noticing that she was telling me things in secret whispers. Then suddenly she announced to everyone, 'OK, who wants a massage?' That sounded good to me, but I didn't want to seem too enthusiastic in case the others got a hint of how keen I was on Katie. So, as usual, I sat back and let everyone else get on with it.

Eventually Katie asked, 'Pete, do you want one?' and I said, 'OK, if it's all right with you.' Now the massage I got was noticeably shorter than the ones Razor or Brocket got, but I had the benefit of a little extra. Katie kept whispering in my ear, hoping the microphones wouldn't pick up what she was saying. She told me, 'I hope you believe me and I hope you trust me. I might not be able to show you in here but when it's over you will know.'

'Why do you have to wait?' I whispered back. 'I don't understand.'

'Because I can't.'

I wondered if that was because she was still feeling some attachment to her boyfriend, Scott, even though she had told me just before we went into the jungle that they had been having some problems and were on the verge of breaking up.

'I think it's over but I needed to come into the jungle to clear my mind and work out exactly what I want to do,' she told me.

'Is this for real?' I asked. 'Do you really feel what I feel?'

'And more,' she replied.

She had asked me if I had a girlfriend, and seemed pleased when I said no. It was one of those rare moments in my life when I didn't have a girl on hand – mainly because, a while back, I'd broken up with my latest girlfriend when I heard her having sex over the phone. Let me tell you the full heartbreaking story.

It was before I went into the jungle that I got the worst phone call a man can ever have. It was from a girl I was seeing at the time, who I've chosen not to name. We'd been an item off and on for a while and there were times when I would say to her, 'I love you but I'm not in love with you.' I was happy but I was honest. I always told her that if I met someone else I would let her know before I would go out on a date with the new woman. It sounds a bit crazy now, but that was the way my mind worked then. Sure enough, we did split up, mainly because I was in Cyprus and she was in England, but we still spoke on the phone from time to time and even though we were apart we still had strong feelings for each other.

I asked her if she had met anyone else but she assured me, 'No way, I'm so in love with you. There's no one else.' She'd constantly call my brothers and tell them, 'You know he's the one for me. I'm going to wait, I don't care, until he gets everything out of his system.'

Just before I went into the jungle, Danny said to me, 'You know what? If this girl is that adamant she's going to wait for you, then maybe she's the one you've been looking for all these years.' He had a point.

So I rang her to tell her I would be in London for a short visit in the near future and suggested we meet. We had to talk to work out if we really did have a future together. She said, 'Oh, baby, I can't wait – I can't wait. You've got to call me when you know the exact date you'll be here.'

So of course I called her. One morning I woke up, felt a bit weird and thought, Maybe I'll give this a real go. It was 9am in Cyprus, 7am in London, so I thought she would still be in bed but wouldn't mind being woken up by my call.

Her phone rang a few times and then went dead, as if it had been answered but then deliberately turned off. That was weird, so I called again. But the same thing happened. I rang a third time and once more it seemed as if someone was answering then turning the phone off. She's either in the toilet or something's going on, I thought. So I decided to ring one last time. The phone rang again and she answered once more, but this time she missed the off button and I could hear her voice. She was moaning, 'Oh... Ooh... Mmmm... Aah...' You don't have to be a genius to work out what she was up to. But, unbelievably, I thought I would give her the benefit of the doubt.

So I held on, but I was stunned to suddenly hear a man's voice. I cut off the phone while I worked out what I should do next.

I rang her again but she wouldn't take the call, so I decided to text her, saying, 'You need to call me now! It's about Sunday.'

Within five minutes she was on the line to me, from a room that echoed just like a bathroom, whispering, 'What's up, baby?'

'Nothing,' I replied. 'I just had this really bad dream that you would cheat on me. But you wouldn't do that, would you?'

'What! Never,' she lied.

'You would tell me if you were with someone, wouldn't you?' I asked. 'I know we're not together right now but we agreed to be honest with each other and I am starting to think you're a special girl. So you would tell me if there was someone else?'

'Baby, of course I would! I love you so much,' she lied again. Then she came out with an even bigger lie. 'Give me ten minutes and I'll be out of the dentist's.'

I couldn't believe she could be so brazen. 'OK, call me

when you're finished,' I said. 'Jeez, I didn't realise dentists opened at seven in the morning in England.'

There was a stunned silence while she tried, and failed, to think of another lie to get her out of the mess she was in. But she couldn't.

'Baby, I've got to go, I'll call you in ten minutes,' she said, and hung up. About 20 minutes later she rang me again.

'Can I ask you a favour about your dentist?' I asked her.

'Yeah.'

'Can you book me in when I come over?'

'Why?'

'Because I want to know if he's going to give me the same pleasurable time that he just gave you.'

There was a silence.

'I don't hate you,' I told her. 'Not only do I not hate you, I forgive you. But I will never forget and you will never, ever hear from me again.'

Bang! That was it. I never spoke to her again. I never texted her again. I never said a word. I was very hurt, but in a way it helped me because it meant that, when the time came to go into the jungle, I went with no strings attached. I was completely single. And that made it so much easier for me when Katie came along and swept me off my feet.

Anyway, back to the jungle. Whatever anyone says about me, I always remained consistent with Kate. I never played any games or messed her about. I knew, given the way she was acting, that people in England were probably thinking I was all over her, like some lost puppy. But I didn't care. I came into the jungle with nothing to lose. I like this girl and she's made it blatantly clear she likes me, I told myself. If she wants to be two-faced, she can, but I know she's only doing it for the camera.

By now I was certain she liked me. I knew that she felt what I felt – from little things, like the way she held my hand in a certain way that said, please don't let me go. Everything about the way we touched was love.

There was nothing sexual. I actually thought, Please, God, don't let her want to jump into bed straight away because I won't like her. I'll be put off.

If you build a relationship on something special it works. Neither of us talked about having sex the whole time we were in the jungle. When she'd get changed everyone would turn and look at her. That made me angry. I thought the guys would give her a bit of respect. Then I'd get upset inside – even though I had no right to step into her life and tell her what to do.

I knew I could be the next to go, but I made a conscious effort not to change my tactics. I just stayed in the background and let Katie run rings round me. The more she publicly snubbed me the more determined I became to be close to her at every opportunity. If she didn't like me sitting next to her – or wanted to give the impression that she didn't – then let her get on with it. It was such a crazy time. When the cameras were on her she'd treat me like dirt. The moment she thought it was safe to let out her true feelings, she'd be begging me, 'Can you please come over and give me a hug tonight when everyone's asleep?'

'Why can't you come over to me?'

'Because I can't.'

'Why, Katie? Why?'

'Well, for a start, we'd probably both kill ourselves falling out of your hammock, you prat.'

'Yeah, I'd forgotten that. But I still don't see why I...'

'Please, can you do it. Please, can you do it?'

Now let me tell you the truth about me and my acorn. After the second time I paid a night-time visit to her bed, she was in a real teasing mood, trying to put me down. I knew she was impressed with my physical appearance, but she just had to tell me, 'You're really small down there. In fact, Pete, it's not even worthwhile going there. You're just an acorn.'

She hadn't got a clue about my size, of course. She just wanted to get one over on me in front of everyone. The tight little shorts I was wearing didn't help, because I had to tuck my manhood away so that when I got a bit excited it didn't become too obvious.

Being told you're small in the trouser stakes is about the most hurtful thing that can happen to a man. But I tried to make it look as if I was taking it in my stride and said, 'Let her make jokes, I know she's really dying to have a look.' Deep down, though, I was angry. I'd been made to look a fool.

But that anger didn't last. How could it when Katie was so sweet to me the next day. 'You know last night, when you came by and you said hello to me when I was asleep,' she said. 'I never wanted it to end.'

'Well, why don't you come to me tonight? It's your turn now.'

'I can't. Please trust me. When this is all over, I'll do everything I promised to do. I'll be all over you. If I don't do that you can just walk away, but you have to give me the benefit of the doubt.'

So what's a man supposed to do? 'OK,' I said. 'I'll come to you again.'

That night I tiptoed over to her bed and slipped under the covers, but she was fast asleep.

'Katie, it's me...'

She woke up slowly, said, 'Oh,' then reached up and caressed my face with her thumb.

'I don't want to be without you, Katie,' I whispered softly, my lips just inches from her ear.

'I don't either,' she said.

And then I kissed her gently on the lips and ran my hand over her body. It was our first real moment of intimacy and I was aroused instantly. The acorn became an oak!

Because it was night I thought no one could see us. What I didn't know was that some of the cameras in the camp were infrared and could pick up images in the dark. We held each other close, our excited bodies pressing close to each other – or as close as you can get with an oak tree in the way – before I kissed her for the last time and whispered, 'Time for me to go, Katie. I love you.'

I slipped out of her bed, adjusted my shorts to take the strain, and that's when I gave the cameras a full frontal of my manhood in all its glory. That night was so special to me because it proved beyond any doubt that Katie did care for me and had the same feelings that I had for her. Being turned on is not just about sex – it's much more powerful, much more satisfying, when it's love for someone else that arouses you. That's exactly how it was for Katie and I. She's the first lady to stimulate my mind as well as my loins (yes, I know that's an Eddie Murphy line from *Coming To America*, but he's welcome to sing my songs if he wants to).

I knew, after that night of magic, that I just had to be patient. But the next day, with the cameras rolling, she just kept on talking about my acorn, and that made me feel ridiculous.

A few days later, when no one was listening, I said to Katie, 'Why don't we go down to the pool and go for a swim – nothing else, we don't have to do anything else. Why can't we go – just me and you?'

She shrugged and played dumb.

'Do you understand?' I asked.

'Yes, I understand,' she said, and bit her lip as if she was upset about something.

She wouldn't talk to me in camp that night and I found out later that she went to Alex's bed and confided in her. Katie believed I had asked her to go to the pool so we could have sex, because that would definitely keep both of us in the show. Nothing could have been further from the truth.

When I found out what was going through her mind, I went straight up to the bush telegraph and said, 'I want to leave. I don't need to win this. I just need her to know that I meant everything I've said to her, that's all I care about.' But they wouldn't let me take the easy way out.

It didn't help when Brocket sat down next to me on a log and said, 'You know I've got to tell you that you've been played...'

'Why?' I said.

'She's been asking me to set her up with one of my mates when I get out.'

It broke my heart. It felt like my first love had just had the life crushed from it. My jaw dropped and I lost all faith in myself and in Katie. I couldn't wait to wake up the next morning and say to her, 'How dare you treat me like this?'

That next day we had it out. We had an argument and I took her away from the camp and said, 'I can't believe the bullshit you've given me. You've made me fall for you and all you're doing is using me like a toy.'

'Whatever! I'm not going to argue about this now,' she said.

'Oh yes you are,' I snapped back. 'Look at the way you're treating me. The whole country's going to think I'm a dickhead. I can't believe you're doing this to me. I haven't tried to sleep with you. I haven't tried to do anything. All I've done is like you. What's wrong with that?'

Obviously the country saw how she was treating me and, for whatever reason, she was voted out that morning. That really shocked me, and the minute she left, instead of going, 'Ha! I got my victory!' I felt devastated. I didn't want to be in that camp any more. That day I lost all interest in the show because I couldn't stop thinking about Katie and how much I wanted to be with her again to prove to her that my feelings were genuine. If I could have one wish, I thought, it would be for her to know the truth. Even if I never got to see her again. That was so important to me.

CHAPTER ELEVEN

IN DEEP

WHEN I FINALLY left the jungle I felt much stronger. I still had all these feelings for Katie, but I was beginning to realise that perhaps she wasn't the right girl for me after all.

My plan after the jungle was to stay in Australia for a few days and spend some quality time with Mum and Dad. After that I intended to head back to Cyprus and the gym I was running. But because of what happened in the jungle, everything had changed. For a start, I couldn't believe I'd actually made it to the final day. Just as I was about to leave, Claire greeted me on the bridge. The producers allowed me to unhook my mike so that we could speak alone for ten minutes. Claire had an urgent appointment in Miami and a helicopter was waiting to take her to the airport.

'Listen, Peter,' she said, holding my arms firmly. 'Remember how much you wanted a second chance?'

Tears started to well up in her eyes. Claire proceeded to tell me about a new album deal, a regional tour and even a calendar. By now I was confused, lost and overwhelmed.

'There's one other thing I have to tell you,' she said. 'Katie has asked me to manage her and I've agreed.'

I was amazed.

'I've seen a new side to her, Pete,' Claire explained. 'What I said before was wrong. She's a really sweet girl and I think she genuinely loves you. How the papers portray her is not true.'

Apparently, Katie's mum, Amy, had been impressed by how hard-working Claire had been throughout the series. While some of the other managers were off enjoying themselves in the bar, Claire was glued to her laptop 24/7.

But, before I had time to let that bombshell sink in, I was whisked off to meet my parents. Katie was with them. When I saw her for the first time with her hair done nicely and with full make-up on, do you know what I thought? Inside I went, Ugh! She was also a bit drunk and I didn't like that.

We cuddled in front of the TV cameras and I whispered to her, 'You see. I told you I wasn't lying.'

In the past 24 hours Katie had watched footage from the show. She saw how I was talking so lovingly about her once she had been evicted and she also saw herself being two-faced about me. Most importantly of all, she heard me telling the others how much I cared about her. Something must have clicked and she decided, This is it!

She could tell I was staring at her face, which was so different from the one I'd become accustomed to in the jungle.

'Don't look at me,' she said.

All I could think to say that wouldn't be too unkind was, 'I think you looked so beautiful in the jungle. I knew it was going to be impossible to beat that look. You looked better in the jungle without the make-up and with the hair off your face.'

I could tell she was a little hurt. 'They've done my hair wrong,' she said. 'I don't usually have it like this.'

Again I wasn't sure where I stood. Was she genuinely concerned that I didn't like the way she looked or was she playing a game, as I suspected she had been doing for the previous two weeks?

Then Claire said, 'Pete, we need to talk.' She explained that my record company wanted to re-release 'Mysterious Girl' and that there could be a lot of work coming up for me in the next few months. I was in a daze.

All the time Katie stuck to my side like glue. It was weird – at times in the jungle she didn't want to know me, but now she wouldn't leave me alone. Was this another game?

Then she leaned close and whispered to me, 'Look, I know you're going to get whisked away to do interviews and I may not see you for a while, but there's one thing I have to say.'

I had no idea what she was talking about.

'It begins with M,' she said, smiling. 'And it's a leap year.'

The only M she could have meant was 'marriage', I thought, but why would she be saying that to me? So I played her along a bit.

'Manchester?

'No. M. Leap year. You know…'

'Manhattan?'

'Pete!'

'Well, what are you talking about?'

'Please,' she said, almost begging me to be serious. 'M. Leap year. Please say yes, please say yes.'

'Marriage?' I said incredulously.

'Yes. Say yes.'

I pretended that the penny was slowly dropping.

'It's a leap year,' she said. 'So I can propose to you. Please say yes.'

I was really confused, but matters were taken out of my hands because Claire insisted that I had to go. It was a circus out there. I was told by Claire that I had a big deal to do exclusive stories for the *Sun* and *Now* magazine and that I couldn't talk to, or be seen with, anyone or it would ruin the deal. They ordered me to stay in my hotel room for 24 hours so that no press, other than the *Sun*, could get to me. If I was pictured anywhere else I might lose my deals with both the *Sun* and *Now*. As I walked off to where our car was waiting, we passed Katie's mum, who looked at me and said, 'What have you done to my daughter?'

I laughed and said, 'What has she done to me!'

My parents were waiting in the car for me, and Dad's first words were, 'Listen, son, we think you should stay away from that girl. She's no good for you. We saw how she treated you.'

There was a girl in the car filming for ITV and as we drove off she turned round and said, 'I've got a CD that Katie gave me. She wants me to play it for you.'

So there I was, squashed in the middle between my parents, when on comes Phil Collins singing 'Against All Odds'. And that was the moment I knew that Katie and I were going to spend the rest of our lives together. Our love really was against all odds. I sat there with the camera on me, looking very solemn. I didn't know how to react – laugh, cry, what? Mum and Dad had no idea how significant the music was; they probably thought it was part of the show. But inside I was in turmoil.

I was in love but trying not to believe it, knowing I'd get hurt. Thinking it was just a waste of time. Knowing everything I'd been through in the past and knowing I couldn't go through it again. But all the time knowing too that Katie is the most special person I've met in my whole life.

Back at the hotel there was a string of messages saying Katie was desperate to see me. The determination of this woman! I couldn't understand her game. She must have called my room about 30 times that day. This was her karma. I couldn't answer the phone, because I wasn't allowed to talk to anybody – not just Katie! She detested Claire for a while because she believed I'd been warned to keep away. Claire needed to fly back for a meeting in Miami and had left her sister, Vikki, in charge until her flight later that day. I love Vikki and I've known her for years. I gave her and her husband Richard one of mine and Gillian's pet dogs, Jack, when I moved back to Australia in early 2000. They still have him.

Katie was trying to contact me, but Claire had left instructions with Vikki not to put anyone through. Even DJ Chris Moyles, who was responsible for the re-release of 'Mysterious Girl', was put straight on to the answerphone! Katie thought Vikki had a personal vendetta against her, but all she was doing was protecting my magazine deals. Katie had been drinking and she was upset and crying. She said a few nasty things about Vikki in her last book and I'd just like to set the record straight. It was nothing personal, Vikki was merely doing what she'd been told and protecting me. She would do the same for Katie and Katie now knows the real reasons behind what Vikki was doing, so it's all sorted.

That night everyone was attending an after-show party for *I'm A Celebrity*... At the last minute I decided not to go. Around midnight Katie turned up at the hotel and started causing a riot. There are certain people who don't know how to control their drink and she's one of them. I'd already been told by the *News of the World* and the *Sun* that, if anyone managed to photograph me with Katie, my exclusive deal would be off. But do you know what? It wouldn't have mattered to me had I known how she genuinely felt about me. In the past I'd always put my career before a relationship – which is why I hurt Kathy, Gillian and many more so much – and I wasn't about to make that mistake again. But, because I thought Katie was playing me about, I refused to make the sacrifice.

She – on the other hand – didn't give a shit about her deal. She was willing to prove her love for me by doing exactly what the papers told her not to do.

About half an hour earlier she'd called my room and Danny had answered. Against everyone's advice, I decided to take the call. 'Peter, please,' she said, but couldn't say any more than that.

'I thought you said in the jungle that you never cry,' I said.

'I don't. But this is different. I've got to see you, I need to see you.'

'Don't mess me about, please,' I quickly told her. 'Why are you doing this?'

'Please, please,' she blubbered. 'Are you going to be there tonight at the after-show party?'

'No. I've been told not to.'

'Oh, Pete, why are they doing this? Why won't they let me come and see you?'

'Look, Katie,' I said, desperately trying to work out how I could break it to her that my parents thought she was bad news. 'I really don't know what the problem is, but I promise I'll speak to you tomorrow.'

'I can't – I'm leaving tomorrow to go back to England.'

I knew I couldn't let her leave Australia without seeing her again. I was in too deep for that. So I ignored everything everyone had told me and said, 'OK, let's meet tonight.'

'Will you be in your room at midnight?' she asked. 'I'm coming up to see you.'

'Fine,' I said. 'See you then.' And I put the phone down. Danny was not impressed.

'Brother, do you know what you're doing?' he demanded.

'Yes, I do.'

Danny thought for a moment. 'Well, you're not a kid any more, you're a man of 31, so I guess you're able to make your own decisions. Just be careful. She can only stay here for a minute or two. And if anyone finds out, I'm not going to be held responsible.'

It was a couple of minutes before midnight when there was a knock at the door and Katie stormed in. She was drunk and rude to everyone. She was wearing a horrible low-cut top and a very short skirt. Her hair was all frizzy and looked a mess. I'm embarrassed to admit it, but I made sure I was in the shower when she arrived. She'd only ever seen me looking grubby and I'd cleaned myself about 300 times. I was in good shape and I'd lost over a stone. I was looking and feeling great.

She walked straight into the bathroom. I only had a towel wrapped around my waist. Her first words stunned me. 'Peter, please marry me,' she sobbed. 'No one wants me to see you, but I'm in love with you.'

She was drunk and I couldn't take her seriously. Judging by the state of her, I doubted a relationship would last more than a week!

Now she started to beg. 'Oh, Pete, please. You've got to say yes, you've got to say yes.'

Then my brother came in from next door and she said, 'Danny, Danny...'

'What?' he replied, not knowing what to make of the bizarre scene before him.

'Pete said yes,' she told him excitedly.

'Yes to what?'

'I asked him to marry me.'

Danny's jaw dropped. He was lost for words. Katie turned back to me and said, 'Pete, say yes in front of your brother.'

So I hugged her and told her, 'Yeah, yeah. Whatever,' hoping it would calm her down.

Suddenly she sobered up. 'What do you mean, whatever?'

'It's cool, cool, cool,' I told her and winked at my brother, indicating with a nod of my head that he should go back to his own room.

Once he'd left, Katie's tears flowed again. 'No, you can't let me go,' she said. 'I've never felt this way about anyone. Never, never, never. Look, I'll prove it to you.'

'Yeah? How?'

'I'll never leave your side... every night... every day...'

I hugged her tight again. But she had one more bombshell up her sleeve.

'Do you want a little suck?'

I couldn't believe what I was hearing. At this point my feelings were all over the place and I didn't know whether to respect her or not. I was shocked, but so turned on and I'm ashamed to say I did take advantage of Katie that night. I'm very clean and I don't like bodily hair, which seemed to impress Katie a lot! Nothing gives a man more confidence than a woman gasping at the size of his assets, and the acorn was once again an oak. She started going down and she was absolutely amazing.

Under normal circumstances I'd have been very shocked at a girl doing what Katie was doing when we'd only known each other such a short time. But then I figured that the two weeks of intensity we'd just spent in the jungle must be equivalent to six months of a normal affair. But after ten minutes she stopped and said, 'Right, that's your lot.' Typical Katie! Why don't you go and kill it, eh?

'I'm not going to sleep with you,' she said.

'Have I asked you to?' I replied.

At that moment Danny knocked on the door and told Katie she would have to leave.

'I want to lie in your arms and stay here all night,' she begged me. 'I'll do anything, anything you want. I'll stay here. If you want, I'll cancel my flight home.'

'No, don't do that. I've got work to do over the next few days, so you'd better go home.' We hugged once more and I kissed her tenderly and said goodnight. As she closed the bedroom door behind her I had such mixed feelings.

'You're not seriously going to marry her, are you?' said Danny.

'She's just mucking around,' I said with a shrug.

But deep inside I wondered if she was. A girl had never ever asked me to marry her. I imagined what it would be like to be inside her. It was the first time I started to really think about her sexually. All night I was in cloud nine.

I knew Katie was flying home early the next morning and I was desperate to speak with her before she left. I needed to know if she really meant everything she'd told me the night before. Already I was missing her desperately. I had a message that she'd tried to call and I phoned her back instantly.

'Hi,' she said, sounding flustered. 'I've got so much stuff to pack and Harvey has been a little shit all morning.'

'Listen, did you mean everything you said last night?' I asked.

'Yeah, of course I did,' she said.

'Ah! It wasn't just because you'd had a few drinks?'

'No, of course not.'

'Right then, give me your mobile number. I'll call you when I get to London.'

She gave me her mobile number before curtly replying, 'OK – see you sometime.' There wasn't a hint of emotion in her voice. I was left holding the receiver, feeling confused. So once again it wasn't happening!

I went down for breakfast and bumped into Angie, the girl I had invited for coffee. She could tell by my face that something was going on, so she asked if I was OK.

'Yes,' I lied. 'It's just that my mind is all over the place because of Katie and I really don't know what to do.'

She smiled and said, 'Just do what you feel is right.'

'But I don't know what's right. I think she's just mucking about and I don't know if she means it.'

'Well, it's not for me to say.'

I thought to myself, What a pity I hadn't had a fling with Angie instead of falling for Katie. Life would have been so much simpler. I kissed her on the cheek and said goodbye. When I got back to my room the first thing I did was check if any messages had been left for me. I was really hoping that Katie would ring me when she got to the airport. But no call came. And I became convinced that everything she had said to me was just bullshit.

That afternoon, while I was doing my interview with the *Sun*, Ariel, the ITV girl who had been doing the filming in the car, rang me and said she had an envelope for me.

'It's a message from Katie,' she said. 'She gave it to me before she left for the airport. She said she wouldn't be able to call you but this letter would explain everything.'

I didn't want the *Sun* to know anything about this, so I asked Ariel where she was. She said she was by the pool and I told her I would nip down a bit later and collect the letter. When the interview was done, the *Sun* wanted to take some more pictures, so I suggested we go down to the pool, which would give me the perfect opportunity to pick up the letter from Ariel. When she gave it to me I couldn't wait to tear it open, so I turned to the *Sun* photographer and said, 'Can you give me a couple of minutes?' He went off to get a beer and I found a quiet corner and sat down to read Katie's letter.

There was a lump in my throat as I read her words. 'You have made my life complete,' she had written. 'You are the only person that's been able to have this effect on me.' It was beautiful. There were another two or three paragraphs which were deeply personal and which I'll never tell a soul about, and she finished by saying, 'Please call me when you get back to London if you want me, because I know you are the one.'

There it was again. The message she had kept whispering to me in the jungle. 'You are the one.' And I was feeling the same way about her. What was going on? Was Peter Andre really in love? Yes he was.

CHAPTER TWELVE

COMPLETE

ON THE PLANE back to London the next day, I sat beside the girl from the *Sun* and she quizzed me about Katie. It was a very difficult time, because the paper was paying me a lot of money for the low-down about what happened in the jungle, but I didn't want to reveal anything that might spoil what I hoped lay ahead between Katie and I. So I tried to just shrug it all off.

'Well, of course I really like her,' I said, which was true. 'I did see her after I came out of the jungle, but I don't suppose I will meet her again.' What a whopper!

Luckily, there was no direct question from the *Sun* about whether Katie and I might be in love, so I didn't have to tell any real lies. Just little white ones.

When I arrived at Heathrow it was mayhem. There were fans screaming and dozens of press people trying to snatch a picture or a few words. But, dazed and confused as I was, I wasn't having any of that, and I was whisked straight off to a waiting limo. My brother met me at the airport and he was just the person I wanted and needed to see. I gave him a quick hug and told him to meet me back at the hotel. The first thing I did when I was alone in my hotel room was to call Katie's mobile, but she had it turned off and I had to leave a message. Several hours passed and she didn't reply, and I couldn't help telling myself, Here we go again. It's another game. This isn't the girl who's waiting for my call!

But, little did I know, Kate was off doing something that I'm happy she does and I know it takes all day – hair salon and nails! That's where she was. Several weeks later, when I eventually went to the salon, everyone told me how gutted she had been. She was having her hair done and her phone was out of service. She didn't realise and was wondering why I hadn't called. She didn't even believe I'd actually called until the message came through a day later.

I sat on the bed and thought it through. Well, you know what you do, Pete. You don't be stupid and throw it all away just because she hasn't phoned. You call her again and give her another chance. Ring her one more time and then, if you get nowhere, that's it. If her phone's still off and it goes to answering service and she doesn't ring you back, forget it. End of story.

I called the number again, and on the third ring she said hello.

'Hi,' I said, trying to be cool, but not feeling it at all.

'I was wondering if you would ring,' she said.

'Well, I did. I left you a message.'

'But I didn't get it... I'm knackered,' she said, changing the subject. 'Are you?'

'Yeah, I've just flown in. I only got back three hours ago.'

'I've just got in from the hairdresser's in Brighton,' she said, as if that could be as tiring as a 22-hour flight from Sydney. 'Do you want me to come and see you?'

'Yes, that would be nice,' I said.

'OK, I'll jump straight in the car and I'll be with you in about an hour.'

I couldn't wait. The first thing I did was have a long shower, then I picked out a nice clean shirt and sat on the bed, as nervous as a groom on his wedding day. When Katie breezed into my room I knew our love was real. She looked wonderful, and when I held her in my arms and we kissed, it was such a special moment.

We sat on the couch, poured a couple of glasses of wine, talked and listened to music. It was wonderful. The whole night was about each other. We talked about how we felt every single day in the jungle.

'Remember that night when it was raining and we had to huddle into the bush telegraph? I was so hoping you'd put your arms around me and keep me warm,' Kate confessed.

'But why did I get the feeling that you didn't even want me to stand next to you? Why were you really close to Razor?'

'I had to act,' she pleaded.

After that, every couple of hours she'd say, 'So are you going to marry me?'

She'd now asked me about 30 times in the past three days. This girl is persistent, I thought, and I finally understood the depth of her feelings and commitment to me. Once everything was out in the open, I said to myself, I *am* gonna marry this girl. *I* am gonna ask her. I won't say yes – *I'll* ask her. But not yet.

We were holding each other so tight and sometimes I'd kiss her on the head and she'd kiss me on the forehead. I looked into those beautiful green eyes and said, 'Come with me.' We stood up and I led her into the bedroom.

Seeing Kate naked for the first time was even better than I expected. It was the first time I'd actually seen her naked, the first time I'd felt how soft her skin was, the first time I got to smell her body. I discovered every inch of her as my hands travelled down her body. I savoured her moment by moment. She couldn't have been more perfect. Her belly button was so gorgeous, the skin around her stomach was so stunning and she had a beautifully shaped waist. There wasn't a blemish on her body. She had beautiful thick lips and green eyes. The only thing that got in the way was... well, how do I put it... silicone. Of course, I've grown to love every part of her and there are no complaints in any way. But even the skin around her breasts was perfect. Nothing about her body seemed anything less than that.

I'd been with plenty of lovers before, but nothing like this. To say Kate is great in bed is an understatement. In the nicest possible way and without sounding crude, I'd like to say that she's the sweetest-tasting woman I've ever had the pleasure of giving pleasure to. She tasted and smelled so beautiful. She was so clean. I was overcome by a mixture of anticipation, anxiety, love, lust – everything rolled into the most amazing sexual experience of my life. I remember looking in her eyes as I was about to climax and cradling her head as the final moment approached. We looked at each other and it was so intense I almost couldn't believe it was real.

I understood what making love was that night. Everything was to do with our feelings. One thing I really enjoyed and wanted her to do was to climax in my mouth. I really, really wanted that and I wasn't going to go anywhere until she did. I wanted every part of her. I remember kissing her feet and how scared she was in case I didn't like anything about her. She was such an unselfish lover and kept trying to satisfy me. In fact, for both of us the whole experience was so selfless – it was all about pleasing each other. We shared a feeling of completeness.

That night we made love for hours, climaxing with the most intense orgasm I have ever experienced. We collapsed in each other's arms and I'll never forget the words she whispered. She held my hand so tight and said, 'The only way this is going to work is we have to be together 24/7. We can't be out of each other's sight. It's the only way.' I knew then that she was committed and to this day we've kept that promise, as much as our working lives allow us to. For months and months afterwards we never let each other go in bed – not even for a second. The only reason we do sometimes now is because this house is so hot. But we always still touch feet or hold hands when we fall asleep. That's our security.

Of course, that amount of commitment was frightening – it frightened me right up until our wedding day! In the past I'd always been selfish in relationships and taken what I wanted. But with Kate it was different. There had been so much confusion and I had a preconceived perception of her. Once I'd been proved wrong, my feelings were even stronger. There was such promise in our relationship and I knew that sex with her would obviously be amazing but I wanted more than that. I wanted to make love in a way that showed just how much we loved one another. I wanted her to break down her barriers and give everything she had always wanted to give. I knew her personality was desperate to come out. She was dying to be this homely person. I could feel it. The conversations and feelings we had were so much more than I'd ever expected.

Once we'd made love that night, I knew that this was it. It was the minute all my priorities changed. This was the first time I let myself go in many ways, even to the point where I didn't want to exercise any more. Kate never liked me just because of my body. It was always a feeling thing. We were physically crazy for each other, but initially I was driven just by her eyes. I know it sounds bizarre. I know what I felt and no one can ever tell me anything different.

The days that followed our reunion in that London hotel weren't easy, because we were still theoretically banned from seeing each other. We talked a lot on the phone but we had to be very careful not to be seen together in public, because the press were just itching to get a shot of us. We were keeping things under wraps and Kate would leave the hotel separately via the underground car park, in a vehicle with blacked-out windows. It was as if we were conducting a hidden romance, which only made our commitment to each other all the stronger.

At first I couldn't see the point. Everyone had seen us

falling in love in the jungle, so why did we have to keep it quiet? But Claire told us, 'The media attention will only make things harder. Build your relationship alone first. If you want people to support your love, keep it to yourselves.'

Of course, she was right. We needed time to strengthen our relationship without public scrutiny. Katie and I are both insecure people and the last thing we needed was ex-lovers selling their stories to the press. By the time we eventually revealed our secret, the media wanted our relationship to work and gave us their support.

A couple of weeks after we'd been together, Katie introduced me to Harvey properly. Up until then she had kept us apart because she was anxious we wouldn't click.

It was true that in the past I'd vowed never to date a woman with a child, but then I'd also vetoed blonde hair and silicone implants. All that had changed now. I loved everything about Katie and I was willing to accept every part of her life.

'If he's from you, I love him,' I told her, and that's how I felt.

In all honesty I couldn't see why I wouldn't love the child. And to this day I can't see why in the world his father doesn't give the kid commitment. I just can't understand it. I don't hate Dwight, because he's co-created such a beautiful child, but I'm disappointed. Yet I'm in no position to tell him what's right and wrong and in the end it's hard for any man to accept another man being with his child. Dwight still has rights. For Harvey's sake I don't want there to be too much animosity between us.

Dwight and I have never had much contact. The few times he did visit I was always nice to him, but then I found him a bit arrogant. Honestly, I'm surprised if he sees Harvey every five or six months for two hours. Could I be away from my son for three days? It would drive me nuts. I am aware of what happened between Katie and Dwight, but there is an innocent child in the middle.

It doesn't bother me that Dwight visits so infrequently, because Harvey calls me Dad and that's what I want anyway. One thing I wouldn't be able to handle is Harvey growing up and calling me Peter. It would feel too impersonal.

When I first arrived at Katie's new house in Brighton it was really dilapidated. Of course, her part of the house was clean, but the rest of it was a building site. She was embarrassed I'd be put off by the house. Quite the opposite – I was impressed! The house was so rundown and I really admired the fact that Katie was living with her son in a place with no carpet so she could keep a close eye on the builders. Why wasn't she staying at her beautiful home in Poynings? It must have been because she wanted me to be part of her new life, and not take me to her past. Here was a woman giving so much love to a disabled son in so much need, and she was in full control. Had I known Katie was so anxious about me meeting Harvey, I would have gone to her home much sooner.

And so we conducted our relationship between Katie's house and my hotel. At the time Katie had a massive dog called Smurf who looked like the dog in *Turner & Hooch* and slobbered everywhere and she would always cook a big spaghetti bolognese for us. Unbeknown to me, Kate kept thinking I wanted to stay at the hotel in London. But, in truth, I didn't want to lean on her.

'I should buy myself a place,' I told her.

One of the biggest surprises to hit me when I left the jungle was a massive tax bill from 1998 for £180,000. I paid it, but it crippled me. I used the money I'd just earned from the show and newspaper deals, but I had to pay tax on that as well. At the time I didn't really care because I was on top of the world and I'd found the woman I loved. Then offers of work started to come in and I began to recoup my losses.

'I don't want to move into your house,' I told Kate with a sense of male pride. 'Either I buy half this house or I buy my own house and we can live between the two.'

I couldn't stay at Kate's house indefinitely, because I'm too proud for that. It wouldn't have felt right. So we came to an agreement where she would keep the house and I would build us a home in Cyprus. I have to have my independence. When we had a pre-nup, I knew the press would say Kate insisted on it. The truth is, I insisted on it – for one reason only. I did it because I wanted her to know that I was marrying her for no other reason but that I loved her. If I didn't earn another penny, I would be entitled to nothing of hers. I insisted on it – in fact, to the point where I had to drag her along to the lawyers. She thought it was because I doubted our marriage would last, but that's the way Kate's mind works!

Even while we've been living here, I've been building my place in Cyprus for us. Remember that plot of land I bought a few years back? Now it was time to put it to use.

We're planning to use the house in Cyprus as a holiday home. We won't move from here in Sussex because we love the countryside. Besides, England has been good to us. Our holiday home is going be the first five-star home in Cyprus! It's all very hi-tech and modern, and at the same time the decor is both very Spanish and oriental-influenced. Part of the ceiling in the living room is a tropical fish tank. I've decorated one of the bathrooms in tiles that are inlaid with a denim effect. These state-of-the-art tiles even have little pink bows on them. That's real Kate! It will be the first house of its kind, for sure. But nothing tacky! The whole place has been decked out to look very classy. The entire house is open-plan, with light spilling in through a dome on the roof. The building is completely surrounded by a two-metre-wide veranda. The views are unbelievable. In the front you have the beach and, behind, the mountains.

My dad was responsible for the design. Mum and Dad left their own massive six-bedroom house on the Nerang River in Australia to live in a tiny apartment in Cyprus and build my house for me – and they won't accept a penny. They've been working on it for almost two years. Now that's what I call love. Thank you, Mother and Father – I will never forget this.

The press say stupid things like, 'Pete wouldn't want to break up with Katie because she brings in all the money', but right now I'm very financially secure. What's especially nice is that for the first time in my life I've got a girl who wants to pay for things, not live off me. We've opened a joint account and use that to buy everything.

We're both independent, but we want to do things for each other. So, instead of buying ourselves gifts, we buy each other gifts. Everything's perfect.

CHAPTER THIRTEEN

FATHER FIGURE

MY BOND WITH Harvey developed quite naturally. For the first month or so I held back a bit. I didn't want to fall too deeply for him and then not have him as my own. I always knew there was more to Harvey than just being Kate's son. I knew Dwight would be involved and I knew the boy's grandmother Amy already played a very important role in his life. Amy takes care of Harvey every day and has travelled all over the country taking him to doctor's appointments and nursery schools.

But you can't help falling in love with him. There's a movie called *There's Something About Mary* and I've always said 'there's something about Harvey', something definitely unique about him. This kid obviously suffers from rare conditions and his sleeping patterns are all over the place. But he could be awake from two in the morning playing with his toys and you won't hear a peep – just an occasional giggle. He has his own language, which we can't always understand. Quite often we can't give him answers to the questions he asks. We don't know what he's asking, but it's as if he's asking the right questions and when he doesn't get the right answers he gets annoyed. He can't communicate all the time, so he shows it through frustration. But he's so fascinating. He's a true Gemini – just like Kate – so one minute he's happy and the next he throws a tantrum.

Initially the doctors said he would never be able to see, but recently Kate and I have both noticed him reach for his bottle. And, recently, he saw a beautiful yellow flower and said, ''Ellow.' Even more recently, he will tell you any colour you put in front of him. Blue is 'boo'; green is 'geeen', red is 'wed'. But there's one colour he does say perfectly... pink! I wonder who taught him that!

We'd go to Toys R Us and fill the trolleys up with anything that might entertain him. Not because we wanted to spoil him, but we felt that if he had limited vision we should at least fill it with everything we could find.

'It's important that he grows up knowing the difference between good and bad and that you can't always have everything you want,' I told Kate.

From the start I was determined to teach Harvey discipline. Kate agreed with me. He can have a million things wrong with him, but he will still understand discipline.

In all honesty, I was never put off by Harvey's disabilities. Somewhat selfishly, I thought there was an advantage in it for me. He'll want more love, I thought, and I've got lots to give. I hope he'll always look to me as a father figure. I don't want our relationship to be half-hearted.

The first time Harvey was really sick was about a year into our relationship. His conditions were getting worse and he was putting on a lot of weight as a result of his medication. At first we were confused and cut his calories down completely. We don't feed him more than any other three-year-old. Often he eats out of habit, not necessarily because he's hungry. Apparently, it's an autistic thing. But he treats food as something pleasurable, so that's why he always wants it. He now weighs six stone – twice the average weight for a child his age. The doctor related it to a constant feeling of aching bones and lethargy. Imagine living like that.

One night, within half an hour Harvey's temperature leaped from totally normal to near fatal. One minute he was playing with his toys and the next he was almost having an epileptic fit. This can happen with Harvey and he could go into a coma, so that's why we need to be with him all the time and carry an emergency injection. I saw him shaking and we called an ambulance immediately. His temperature was 39 degrees. Above 40 is fatal.

I held Harvey, tears rolling down my face.

'Please say something – please!' I begged him.

'D-da-da,' he mumbled.

It broke my heart. All I could think was, My son, my son. At that moment I knew I couldn't lose him. By now he was drifting in and out of consciousness and the nurses had placed an oxygen mask on him. Kate went to the hospital in the ambulance and I followed in my car. Harvey stayed in for two nights and it was a horrible time. That was my first glimpse of what Katie's life was like, and what our new life would be like. I understand why people love and relate to her

– she's a successful businesswoman, but she's also a mother who goes through heartbreaks. It's tough. She has pre-programmed in her head exactly what medicines Harvey should take at exactly what times. At times she's a very untidy person, but she's also very smart and when it comes to Harvey absolutely nothing slips her memory.

In the early days I found it very difficult to understand Harvey's illness. I was starting to love him more and more but he wouldn't give me any love in return. I'd walk in the room and sit next to him and he'd push me away many times, as he has done with his mum. It was really disheartening. He can also throw major tantrums. He'll throw his head back, flail his arms, slap, kick and headbutt things. The worst he's done is kick his mother in the stomach and punch her. He's so strong. There have been times when I've had to hold him down with all my strength. We call him 'the little sumo wrestler'!

One night he became so aggressive with his mum that she broke down and started to cry.

'It's all becoming too much,' Kate sobbed. 'He's so aggressive. Some of the schools are refusing to let him in because they think he's too violent!'

Even today, if any other kids come near Harvey he goes nuts. But when he's in a good mood he can be the best kid in the world. We've enrolled him at two schools; one is a special-needs school and the other is for normal children.

As soon as Junior was born we sensed a change in Harvey. He became very jealous and opposed to him. He'd say Junior's name and we'd think, How sweet! But then he'd go for him. He sensed the love was being spread. I'm still

Above left: The big announcement – Katie and I get engaged!

Above right and below: My engagement party on board the Navigator of the Seas. *From left to right*: my best friend Reno Nicastro, my brothers Mike, Andrew, and Chris, and my other best friend and best man George Nicolaou.

All our dreams came true on our fairytale wedding day.
Above: With my parents and, *below*, the proudest man on the planet with his groomsmen.

Above: Happy families – with my parents and my in-laws, Amy and Paul.

Below: Bon voyage to the newlyweds. I jokingly called it our 'moneymoon' but for most of it our honeymoon was an utterly private time in the Maldives, our favourite place in the world.

With my gorgeous baby, Junior, who I love with every bit of my heart. Check out those tiny toes!

My first-ever family Christmas. Since I've been with Katie, I've really started to enjoy the festive season.

The proud father. Kate and the children have given me everything I need to be happy.

Below left: Like father, like son. People say that Junior is my spitting image – he has exactly the same cheekiness as me!

Below right: With Harvey. Despite Kate's initial concerns, Harvey and I get on brilliantly – as soon as we met, something clicked between us.

Above: Happy first birthday, Junior!

Below: Claire, myself and Neville (my co-manager) enjoying ourselves at Elton John's infamous White Tie and Tiara Ball.

My life has had its highs and lows, but I feel like I've finally arrived where I'm supposed to be.

frightened to leave Harvey on his own with Junior. That can't happen for a long time. The only way they can be left in the same room is if one of us is present or Junior is in his playpen, because then Harvey can't touch him. Kate has been teaching Harvey to be gentle whenever he goes near Junior. He'll touch him gently and we'll say, 'Good boy', but then he tries to hit him. Sometimes he only hits him lightly, but sometimes he hits too hard. It felt like more than just sibling rivalry, it felt dangerous at times.

'We're going back to the doctor,' I told Kate. 'We need to do something. We can't leave him and Junior in the same room together and they're brothers – they should be getting on!' In fact, we took him to several different doctors, but none of them could give us any answers. It was a very frustrating time. Amy took a lot of responsibility for Harvey's well-being and I started to feel as if maybe it wasn't my place to give an opinion. I thought I should back off, but I was getting too attached to him and it was a really confusing time for me.

Eventually he began repeating what we'd tell him to say, but it seemed to me and Kate that there was no way he really knew what he was saying.

'He doesn't love me,' I'd complain to her. 'He doesn't even know who I am.'

'Well, how do you think I feel?' she'd say. 'I'm his mother!'

It would break our hearts because he wouldn't give us one bit of love.

Harvey was piling on the pounds and eventually Kate couldn't lift him any more. I began to resent the hospitals. As much as they were trying to do the right thing, Harvey was their guinea pig. They didn't know exactly what was wrong and had to do various tests on him. They informed Kate she'd need to give him an injection every night until he's 18. Harvey has three lots of medication a day, syringes squirted in his mouth – and all before he can even eat anything! Medicine is the first taste he experiences every single day of his life. Then, to top it all off, we have to inject him every night. Initially it was really tough to watch that needle go in. He'd scream the house down.

'I'll do anything,' I told Kate. 'But I can't give him the injection. I don't feel I have the right.'

I'm not sure if she understood what I meant. Although I now thought of myself as Harvey's dad, I still wasn't his father.

Over time I was starting to lose hope that Harvey would ever be normal. I was also growing increasingly concerned for Kate's safety. I was worried that in her stubbornness she would try to lift him when I wasn't around. Harvey is far too heavy for her tiny frame. We talked to everyone – the doctors, the two nannies we have to help with the boys, Kate's mum – and one day it was agreed that we should try the whole 'naughty step' approach. When Harvey is bad we tell him, 'No, don't do it again or you'll go and sit on the naughty step!' Then, if he does it again, we'll either give him one more chance or take him to the step.

'You sit there until you're ready to behave!' we tell him.

Hand on heart, it has made a world of difference. Now he even goes to the naughty step of his own accord if he needs to calm down. These days his temper tantrums aren't so frequent; instead of 20 a day he has three or four. The problem is, when he does have a tantrum they're always really extreme. It's scary to watch and you have to move everything out of the way. He becomes a dead weight and he will not help himself. He gets into a real state and his temperature soars. That's when it's hard.

In time Harvey slowly started to communicate with us. He'd reach for his bottle and say, 'Bot, bot' or 'dink' instead of drink. Then one day, out of the blue, the strangest thing happened. I walked into his room to check on how he was doing. Usually I'd say something like 'Dada' and he'd repeat the word back to me. I'm not sure if he really understood what it meant or even associated it specifically with me.

On this occasion I didn't say a word. I was about to say, 'Oh my God, what have you done to this room?' because the place looked a tip. But before I could open my mouth Harvey looked up and said, 'Daddy.' My heart melted. I can't describe the feeling. That was the moment I knew he was mine. Immediately I ran downstairs to tell Kate.

'You're not going to believe this,' I shrieked. 'He just called me "Daddy" – without me even telling him.'

We both ran upstairs to see if Harvey would do it again. I wanted to make sure he wasn't just using it as a general response to anyone who walked in the room.

When Kate walked in the room he said nothing. Then I walked in and he said, 'Daddy' again. I made Kate repeat the experiment several times and we always had the same result. I was on cloud nine! Straight away, I was on the phone to my parents in Cyprus.

At first Kate was a bit upset. She was gutted that Harvey hadn't called her 'Mummy' first.

'Oh, he doesn't love me,' she sighed.

'Don't be stupid,' I said. 'He loves you more than me! He's acknowledging me because I've been strict with him!' Well, that was my way of thinking.

It was true. I'd always been firm with Harvey. Every time he did something bad I'd say, 'No', but if he did something good I'd cuddle and praise him. 'You are a champion,' I'd tell him. That always made him smile. He quickly learned that good behaviour would earn him a hug. Even Kate can't believe how much he listens to me. It's almost as if he knows he can't get away with temper tantrums in front of me. The only problem was, it made him play up more to his mum, because she takes a very gentle approach in caring for him.

But Harvey was progressing quickly. Within a week he was calling Kate 'Mummy'.

I honestly don't mind Harvey travelling everywhere with us. Having him with us is a blessing. I love him to bits! My only fear is that one day he'll grow up and reject me as a father. He does have abnormalities, but he's still a very intelligent boy. It does scare me that he might reject me, and that's the final barrier I have with him. I give him so much love but I always have the idea in the back of my mind that he's going to leave me. That's the truth. But it won't make me love him any less.

CHAPTER FOURTEEN

WILL YOU...?

A FEW MONTHS after Kate and I had been together, I decided it was finally time to propose. Even though I've done so many predictable things, I hate them! For instance, it was so predictable that I'd release 'Insania' and 'Mysterious Girl' after I'd been in the jungle. I have the same problem with birthdays but always try my best to think of original things to do. I wanted my proposal to be special because Kate had asked me every day for the last few months 'Will you marry me?'

I felt so flattered that she kept asking me. I've never had anyone be so consistent and persistent with me. I knew her birthday was coming up on 22 May, but to propose on that day would be too predictable. I'd already bought the ring, so I was just waiting for the right moment.

A month before her birthday Claire showed me a picture of a ring. 'What do you think of this?' she said.

'Oh, it's stunning. But will Kate love it?'

'I know she will, because I showed her the picture.'

So Claire played a big role in my plans to propose to Kate. She told me I could get the ring from Bill Forman, who ended up making our wedding rings. He used to work for Asprey, but now he's semi-retired and just does things for friends. He is a great jeweller and a good friend. The ring was all white diamonds surrounding a big pink stone.

Her birthday was fast approaching and I couldn't wait. But I had a plan. I decided to give her three surprises to distract her attention from the real gift I intended to offer. I planned to give her the first gift on Friday, then on Saturday morning, the day of her birthday, I'd present her with another. Later that day she'd have a third. Finally, on the Sunday morning, I'd wake up and ask her to marry me.

I knew she really wanted a little chihuahua she could carry around with her. I checked everywhere and a girl who was working here at the time looking after Kate's horses said she'd found an ad for a puppy in a local paper. She said the seller wanted quite a bit of money, but I didn't care even if they were scamming us.

'Let's just go and get it,' I said.

I should have gone on Friday morning, but the girl kept delaying me and it was about 6.30pm by the time we left. She said the house was in Kent, only about an hour from our house. So when Kate came home from work I told her I needed to pop out. She didn't know why I had to go out and thought it was all a bit strange. 'He never goes out and now he's going out with the horse girl. How bizarre.' I asked Kate's sister to come along too.

Four hours later we were in Kent. I don't know where this girl took me, but we got completely lost. We kept ringing the people's number and they said it was fine. But by ten at night they'd switched off their phone and our calls were diverted to the housekeeper.

'It's not a problem. Just get here when you can,' she told us. We eventually arrived at midnight, some six hours after setting out. Meanwhile, Kate was sending me constant messages asking where the hell I was. But I didn't want to tell her and spoil the surprise.

We arrived at the house and pressed the bell. It was a massive farmhouse with big metal gates, and the owner came over to these.

'Who the fuck are you?' he snarled.

'I've come to pick up the dog,' I said, now extremely tired and a little fed up.

'Are you joking? At this time of night?'

Already things weren't going to plan.

'I've got the cash in my pocket,' I said, hoping he would just take the money and hand over the puppy.

'Look, mate, I don't give a fuck about your money. My wife's asleep and she's tired. And you're waking up the other animals in the house.'

By now I was getting desperate. I'd come all this way and I couldn't go back home empty-handed and spoil Katie's birthday.

'I'm really sorry, mate, but we've been ringing.'

'You should use your common sense!'

'Look, I've got the money on me. Do you want it or not?' I said, making one last attempt to clinch the deal.

'You can take your money and shove it up your arse,' the man said, still behind the gates at this point.

'Really!' I said. I couldn't believe his nerve. 'All right – no worries.' I looked at his house number and said, 'I know where you are now, so that's fine.'

'Excuse me – you know where I am?' he said, his fists clenched. 'Do you know what I've got to say about that?'

'Whatever, mate!' I replied. I'd had enough of him.

Suddenly he turned and went into his garage as if to pick something up. I was pretty convinced he was reaching for a shotgun.

'Get in the car now,' I screamed at the girls. 'Let's get the fuck out of here! This guy's going to pull out a gun.'

Kate's sister was freaking out as we drove off at high speed.

'Why did you bring us here?' I said to the stable girl. 'This place is in the middle of nowhere and this guy's a psycho!'

Then I looked in the rear-view mirror.

'Call the police now!' I said.

The man was flying down the road, dodging cars and forcing them into lay-bys. I was in a car with screaming girls, feeling completely responsible for their safety. The madman had caught up with us and was trying to run me off the road. We came to a roundabout, where he went one way and I went the other. To my horror, he'd blocked me off. Another car appeared and blocked us off from behind – it was his mate in a big four-wheel-drive.

As he stepped out of the car I thought, I'm finished now!

'What do you want with me?' I pleaded.

There must have been a minute's delay between him

rummaging around in the car and a police car turning up. I don't know what he was planning to do. I dread to think about it. But the cops arrested him. They handcuffed me but let me go when I told them what had happened.

'Just because of who he is, he thinks he can get away with it!' the man told the police before turning to me with anger in his eyes and threatening, 'This isn't over.'

The cops stayed with him for about 15 minutes and then left. They came to see me the next day and asked if I wanted to press charges. I thought about it but decided not to because I thought the whole episode might come back to haunt me and I didn't want anyone hurt.

That night I arrived home in the early hours after one of the worst experiences I'd had since returning to England. Kate had the hump with me because I'd been out all evening. She had no idea what I'd been up to and she couldn't get hold of me on the mobile. I couldn't tell her the truth for fear of spoiling her other surprises. I simply told her I'd explain later and we had a massive argument. But the first part of her birthday was a shambles.

On Saturday morning, the morning of Kate's birthday, I had an appearance on *CD:UK*. I told Kate I needed her to come with me, but she'd had very little sleep the night before and said she felt knackered.

'Please come!' I begged her, before kissing her on the head and wishing her happy birthday.

In the end she agreed. That night I had a gig in Leeds, so I asked her to come up. It was stupid of me. I should have cancelled it. She was really tired and hardly in the mood to be dragged around. So far, poor Kate wasn't having much of a birthday!

On the way up we stopped off in London for a meal at the Savoy. It was a really uppity place and I would never normally take Kate there. She said it was nice, but I knew inside she thought it was way too posh. By taking her I'd wanted to throw her off the trail of what I was really trying to achieve. Our next stop was in the West End, right outside *The Lion King*. Kate had never seen a theatre show before, so I decided to take her as a treat. It was all VIP treatment – champagne, the works. She was truly blown away by the whole experience.

Then, in the car on the way up to Leeds, I decided to test the strength of her convictions just one final time, however cruel it may have been. Don't forget, she put me through hell for a whole two weeks in the jungle!

'I don't know, Kate,' I sighed. 'I think you still love being this Jordan character. Maybe you need to live like that a bit more. I don't know if we should be together.'

It was all a test to see how she would react. Looking back, I now admit it was a bit stupid! It was her birthday, after all, and so far all I'd managed to do was wind her up! By the time we reached Leeds she really had the 'ump with me (as she would put it). I'd already arranged with the hotel to put roses on the bed in the shape of a heart. I hoped they would distract her from what I was still trying to do. I also ordered pink champagne and a lot of cute little toys – no, not those kinds of toys!

Because of events the night before and the fact that I'd upset her by testing her so much in the car, I decided to bring forward my proposal. So it ended up being the predictable event I'd so desperately tried to avoid. In the circumstances, however, I had no choice. She was getting ready to say, 'Forget it, I'm not coming to the show tonight.'

I poured her some champagne, said happy birthday and kissed her.

'You've been so mean to me,' she whimpered.

'Actually,' I said, 'there's something on my mind.'

'What now?' she sighed.

'Come here. Please,' I said, beckoning her forward to a spot where the light was perfect. 'Just stand here.'

Then I opened the ring case, looked up at her and said, 'Will you?'

She didn't say a word. She was completely gone – confused because of the way I'd been with her all day.

'I'm sorry, Kate,' I said. 'I was just testing you. I just needed to know that you genuinely wanted to be with me, one last time.'

'Yes!' she screamed, before flinging her arms around my neck and showering me with kisses. She absolutely loved the ring. Then I took her to the bathroom, where the light was even better, and I said, 'Can I do it again?' So I got down on one knee and did it again. Then I took her to another part of the room where I thought the light might be better. I asked her to marry me three times in one night.

We didn't officially announce our engagement until October. For the time being we decided to let just close family and Claire and Neville (Claire's partner and my co-manager) in on our happy secret. To my disappointment, when we were filming the first series of our show *Jordan and Peter Laid Bare* the TV people made me re-enact my proposal as they wanted to start the show with this sequence. Otherwise, everything else in that programme was spontaneous and true. I told them it would look stupid, but they insisted. Kate was being really sarcastic and saying, 'Go on, put it on! Not that finger, you idiot!' That spoiled the whole feeling of what had actually happened.

Now we were engaged, everything became a bit more concrete and our relationship felt a lot more solid. I believed that Kate really wanted to be my wife and spend the rest of her life with me. That night we went to the club in Leeds where I was performing. Now that I was engaged to Kate, I became instantly overprotective. For a moment my insecurities crept back and I thought, I hope she doesn't stuff me around now because she's got what she wanted.

I noticed a guy in the crowd dancing with his shirt off. He was obviously a dancer and had a great physique. He stood out like a sore thumb! I was on stage and I could see Kate bowing her head with a coy smile, always looking in his direction. I was getting really wound up because she wasn't looking at me! I was thinking, I've just proposed to you! We had a big argument about it.

Later, when I went down to where she was standing, I realised she couldn't have seen him because there was a massive pillar in the way. In actual fact, she'd been trying to hide from fans who were calling out her name. A girl like that, who's sought after by so many people, could take advantage of her situation. But, to be entirely truthful, my jealousy really stemmed from an element of not trusting myself, because I could remember what I had been like a few years earlier.

I'd shown Kate's mum the ring about a month beforehand and asked for her blessing. But I didn't tell my parents until two months after I proposed because I wanted them to meet Katie first. I wanted them to see her, to know that I was in love, to understand the woman I'd fallen in love with. I did want their approval – because my family are my life. But I didn't want to do it over the phone. I preferred to tell them in person.

It was two months before I took Kate to meet my parents in Cyprus. That was the first holiday we spent together. We were also doing a photo shoot as part of a deal with *OK!* magazine. My manager Claire had gone to great lengths to keep the whole thing secret. *OK!* wanted complete exclusivity on shots. To lay a false trail, Claire had even told one wardrobe assistant we were flying to Barbados. Would you believe it, the next thing we heard was that the *Sun* had sent a photographer out there. You have to be so careful whom you trust, that's all I can say! Anyway, Kerry-Ann Keogh is our stylist now. She's been with us ever since.

We were in the middle of shooting some pictures on the beach when Claire received a phone call warning her that several *Sun* photographers had boarded a plane to Cyprus. It was a race against time. We quickly hired two speedboats, and I remember Claire did a cash deal on the spot to get them. Within minutes we were speeding off to another beach. We were even forced to switch hotels. But *OK!* got their exclusive in the end.

Kate says she was nervous about meeting my parents for the first time, but imagine how I felt. All Mum and Dad knew was the way she had treated me in the jungle. Naturally, they felt protective towards their youngest son. It's the only time I've ever fought for a girl. At first they thought my relationship with Kate was just a phase I was going through. I never went out with blonde girls, I never went out with a girl who had silicone implants. I was very into brunettes and Mediterranean-looking girls. So, when my parents saw Kate with her bright blonde hair, silicone assets and a child from a former relationship, they were quite shocked. When I told them I was in love with her, they thought I must be joking. Directly after I left the jungle, I even remember Mum telling me never to bring her to the house. But it had nothing to do with the way she looked – it was just the way she had treated me.

Parents are always protective of their children. Right at the start of our relationship, I saw an article in which Katie's mum was quoted as saying, 'Oh, God, it'll never work between them. He's not her type.' I can understand why Amy should have been so wary about me. But now we have learned to respect each other and I was thrilled when she said to me one day, 'This is the first time since Katie's been old enough to be out of my sight that I can sleep at night.' That was a very special compliment which I appreciated very much.

Katie's younger sister, Sophie, who's a great girl, said to

me in the early days, 'Pete, I'll like you, as long as you don't hurt my sister.'

I said, 'I promise you that if anyone's going to hurt anyone, she'll hurt me first. I'm in this for a long time, not just for a good time.'

But, once Mum and Dad met Kate, they fell in love with her straight away. We stayed in Cyprus for three or four days and they were so hospitable. In the days leading up to our trip I'd been so anxious. I kept thinking, Please, can everything be right! Kate does mention in her book that our families are very different and they are. There are things I don't necessarily agree with in her family, as I am sure there are things she doesn't agree with in mine, but it doesn't mean I have to go into detail like she did. I respect Kate's family, and Amy is a fantastic grandmother to Harvey. But, believe me, I've had my issues! Still, I suppose most families do.

We were never consciously trying for a baby, but I'll admit we were never 100 per cent careful. Actually, I often find it hard to climax while making love. If Kate had specifically asked me to make her pregnant, it might have taken me two or three days to actually finish the job! Now that we're married I feel it's normal to climax with my wife. It's a psychological thing. When I was engaged I never felt right, but, when I did finish, it would be inside her. So we knew there was always a chance. What I didn't realise is quite how fertile she is. She fell pregnant pretty much straight away. It seemed almost impossible.

Kate kept using pregnancy tests because she was getting broody. But I thought the chance of us actually having a child so soon was pretty slim. We talked about children the first few nights we got together, but I was always a bit scared. You should be married, I thought, and I wanted time to pass so as to make sure she wasn't going to mess me about. Every time she would test negative, so I didn't think any more about it. We probably made love 20 or 30 times and of the three times in that month that I climaxed only once was inside her.

On one occasion we were lying in bed and she pulled out a testing kit. Neither of us thought there was the remotest chance she was pregnant, so we didn't take it too seriously. Then suddenly Katie gasped and said, 'Pete, is that a cross in the middle?'

I looked at it and said, 'No, that's just a line.'

'Yes, but it's got another faint line going across it.'

'No, that's too faint, it doesn't mean anything.'

Then she screamed, 'Pete, I'm pregnant!'

'Oh, shut up, will you,' I said. 'You can't be. Try another test and you'll see I'm right.'

So she did another one – and this time the faint line was much darker.

'I *am* pregnant!' she said.

'Stop pissing about,' I said, cracking a particularly bad joke.

'Pete, I'm not,' she insisted.

'Do it again,' I said. 'I want to watch to make sure you're not winding me up.'

So she did. And I watched. And it was dark blue again. In all, I made her do nine tests before I believed the great news. Poor girl! Every time the line was darker. Peeing nine times in a row is bloody hard.

We didn't announce the news publicly until March the following year. Harvey was sick at the time and we thought it best to wait until he was well again. Kate made an appearance on *GMTV* and we broke the news hours later, after an important scan to make sure everything was OK.

It took months to sink in that I was actually going to become a father. But that night I promised her that I would stick by her every minute and that I'd make her feel so comfortable throughout the pregnancy. There's one other thing I agreed with her that I wish I never had. It was the start of my little downfall.

'Do you know what would make me really happy?' she said.

'What, baby?'

'Comfort-eat with me.'

That was the day the takeaway food started, the day the cooking slowed down and it was just eat, eat, eat. I started eating twice as much as I'd normally eat and it was all junk. How much I'd changed! Ten years ago I wouldn't even have dreamed of eating a biscuit with my tea. Now I was getting through a packet every night.

Kate's biggest craving was ice cubes. The advantage was that it was the only time she ever drank water. She never was a big drinker of water and she still isn't. Throughout a pregnancy hydration is really important. She would eat bucketloads of ice day after day, so I figured that, if she was getting two or three litres of water inside her, that was brilliant.

We'd order tons of food, but she'd only nibble at it. I, on the other hand, would have to eat it all because after all those years of denying myself I was loving the taste of food.

I became a binge eater. I only ever do things to complete extremes! Even if I did start cooking at home, it was takeaway-style cuisine. The more I was eating junk the more I wanted it. I trained less and less. I ate more and more. In four or five months I put on a stone, which I'd never done before. I was always ripped and cut. Now I let myself go completely.

I felt so sad about that, and I still find it hard now to believe that I can get back to what I was. Kate keeps a picture of me in my abs days pinned to the fridge to deter me from eating too much. Actually, it just makes me feel even more depressed! But I'm restarting full training, so by the time this book is out I hope to be back in shape.

Once Kate had given birth, she was able to switch back to normal eating. I couldn't. I craved pizzas and everything I shouldn't eat – ice cream and chocolate. Then I thought, Don't blame Kate. She asked you to comfort-eat but you could have said no. I suppose I was just so happy that she was pregnant and that we were going to have a child.

It was my contribution to the pregnancy, an enjoyable contribution though.

In the day I'd be OK and keep a lid on the eating. I'd get up and have my espresso, because that's standard. Then at lunchtime I'd have a sandwich or something else really moderate. Come the evening, though, when I was least active, I'd go berserk. First, I'd order a massive takeaway – sometimes two full plates with everything imaginable! Then I'd have a tub of Ben and Jerry's or Häagen Dazs ice cream. I'd easily put away one and a half of those. Finally, I'd tuck into a packet of biscuits with a cup of tea – a packet and a half was standard. Then I'd get excited and order pizzas for the next day!

The nights were killing me. It was a vicious circle where I became depressed because I was eating and I was eating because I was depressed. Is this karma again? I asked myself. Is this God's way of punishing me for all those years when I looked at others and thought, How could you let yourself go like that?

After Kate released her fitness video in December, I became down because everything in my life was perfect except for my control of food. I thought, How can such a beautiful woman stand next to such an ugly man? I felt so unattractive. Every time I planned to start on a diet, Kate would say, 'Don't be stupid, just eat with me tonight.' She can eat junk and lose weight. I can't. I used to have her metabolism when I was 27, but I'm 33 now. Everyone said it would change when I was 30 but I didn't believe them. I was angry that I trained all those years and in one year I could lose it.

I don't have the same motivation and drive to go to the gym that I used to because I'm content. I'm going to do it because I want to stand next to my wife and have people go, Wow, look at them! I don't feel the need to strip off in a video clip now, but I guess if I had to do it I would. I just want my wife to have the best man that she can have. I'm training but I'm not as crazy as I used to be. I refuse to beat myself up about it. I've told myself, See this as a lesson to learn that you can lose things. Don't think you're invincible.

During Kate's pregnancy I couldn't help touching her stomach. I didn't want to be a cluggy father, but I still felt very protective towards her. I didn't treat her like an invalid, though, and I thought it was good for her to do some exercise.

I was disappointed in myself that Kate fell pregnant before we got married, because I really wanted to do it the so-called right way. But another nine months without Junior? I don't think I could have handled it. I was ready because I love that child with every bit of my heart.

I know Kate has had an abortion in the past and personally I would never consider it an option. However, I think it's very chauvinistic for a man to dictate what a woman should do with her body. The mother, and the mother only, should make that choice. It's her body. I've appreciated my own mother a hundredfold since I've seen what Kate went through with her first pregnancy. She bore all the pain, the sickness and the mood swings. Then she went through all the pain of labour, only for some man to walk away and demand rights after the event!

To me, rearing kids is either done properly or not at all. My outlook is straightforward. Love and truth are very simple. Marriage, children, family together equal happiness. That's how I see it. I don't like the in-betweens. I know some relationships are less good than others but I also know that as parents you have to sacrifice a lot for your kids. If you get to a point where you have to suffer, suffering for your children is worth it. I can't predict the future, but I know I've married Kate for life – not just to see how it goes for a year or two. We are happy and in love.

Our pre-natal classes consisted of TV shows on the Discovery and National Geographic channels. We watched every programme about prenatal issues and birth. I know it sounds lazy, but we did everything in the comfort of our own home. I probably sound like a bit of a nerd, but it was so important to us to watch and learn. Next time, though, I think we should go to prenatal classes. There's no reason why we shouldn't and we could learn so much more. But I'll never tell Kate what to do. The stress she carries can be enough at times, and she doesn't need me adding to it. I need her to be the most relaxed and comfortable she can be. If that means sitting at home and pigging out on ice cubes, then so be it.

Our sex life had been wild before the pregnancy, and I mean wild. In Kate, I felt as if I'd met my match. We are both fantasists. There's a saying that anything goes in the bedroom only. Stories, fantasies, thoughts – that's where you live them out. We're both very open-minded and experimental and there are no barriers. I couldn't even begin to tell you the kind of things we do together. She's the first person that I've wanted to share experiences on that level with. There were other women who liked to experiment, but it was never love. When you love someone and you like to experiment, wow!

Our lovemaking entered a whole new dimension. People talk about tantric sex and the *Kama Sutra*, but we've reached our own unimaginable levels. Tantra Sutra; Jordandre ultra! We've created two techniques that only we will understand. Just tell her to remember rock climbing and the prayer. She'll laugh when she reads this! Kate, are we going to pray tonight? She knows what I mean!

When Katie first met me, she was a bit freaked out

because she thought that, if she was wild in bed and had these weird fantasies, I would be put off. She was so surprised when she told me what she wanted to do and I said, 'Is that all? You should hear what I've got in mind.' That was when she knew she had found somebody she could be at ease with. It's important to realise that fantasy is just that – you seldom act it out for real. And very often the thought of something is more exciting than the reality.

I could have looked at Kate and thought, Oh, so she's that experienced, huh? But that's not the case at all.

I'm glad she's finally allowing all her thoughts to come out. I don't believe that with any of her exes she's done half the stuff we've done together. Maybe I'm being naive, but I can almost guarantee that she didn't, because the same feelings weren't involved. Had she felt that way with anyone else, she would have married them.

But as soon as Kate fell pregnant, the sex stopped. It was really sudden. Before, it had been wild and passionate exchanges. Now it was as if she was a totally different person. I think it was that lack of sex drive that first raised her suspicions about being pregnant. She couldn't understand it. It did cross my mind that she'd gone off me or was interested in someone else. Then I thought it was me. I do have quite an emotional side to my personality and I couldn't understand what I was doing wrong.

Suddenly, I felt as if I'd been put on a crash diet or was being made to suffer cold turkey. It went on for what felt like an eternity. But I never argued with her about it and it never became an issue. This happens, I thought. I had to, otherwise it would have driven me nuts. I talked to my brothers about it because they're all older than me and have experience of these situations. There are guys who don't like to admit certain things, but it doesn't trouble me. One thing I have learned since my breakthrough is, let everything out – it's OK. It doesn't matter. People will always respect you a whole lot more. If I had to be patient, I would be. Sex was just a part – albeit a wonderful part – of our relationship. Any problems that might arise we would work through together.

CHAPTER FIFTEEN

FAMILY MATTERS

MY FAMILY HAVE always played an important role in my life. One of my greatest hopes – and the source of later disappointments – was that my family and Kate's would hit it off. Don't get me wrong, there's no animosity between them and they all get along quite well. The problem is, they're like chalk and cheese, as I would find out the hard way!

As a celebration for our engagement, Kate and I decided it would be a good idea to take our families on a Caribbean cruise. At the time she was five weeks pregnant and we were keen to keep it a secret. With Kate experiencing her first bouts of morning sickness, that wouldn't be easy.

No one knew about the pregnancy. The only person I told was my brother Chris. We're extremely close and I share everything with him. Claire only found out in February 2006. At the time Kate was competing in the heats to find Britain's entry for the Eurovision Song Contest and she was worried Claire might try to stop her if she knew she was expecting.

We all arrived in Miami to board the cruise ship. Kate and I were both desperate to have a scan of our unborn baby. We were so impatient and couldn't bear to wait until we arrived back home.

Kate grabbed a phone directory from the hotel and we looked up the nearest medical centre. We called a couple of places, but you needed to book an appointment. We wanted something now. At last we found a place. The cost didn't matter. We had an hour and a half to get it done – if that. We told everyone we were getting Harvey a new buggy because the wheels on his old one were broken. We found the hospital and it was really dingy. Kate was given a scan, which showed something like a tiny little ball of fluid. I still couldn't believe it was real. Kate was really excited and loved how the scan looked.

The doctors told us she was already six weeks pregnant. We didn't know if it was a boy or a girl. I wanted to find out, though if we ever have another child I won't. We were told it would be 21 weeks before the sex would be clear. Unbeknown to us, the nurse who later took scans in London knew it was a boy at 12 weeks, because Junior was such a big fella! That made me very proud, of course.

But now, with only 20 minutes left to spare, we had to hurry back to the ship and we still needed to pick up a buggy. Back on board we were desperate to show our families the scans. On the cruise I did tell my brothers about Kate's pregnancy, because it was such a big thing for me. All my life it had been something I'd wanted to achieve. To me, getting married and having kids is the ultimate achievement. I also wanted to prove to Kate that I could tell my friends and family secrets and that they'd never tell anyone.

Unfortunately, the cruise was a disaster. I wish we'd never gone. I had such high expectations about the holiday and none of them materialised. I'd tried to put two very different groups of people together in the hope that they might bond. To my disappointment, it didn't happen and I was deeply hurt. In addition, poor Kate really suffered from sickness a lot of the time.

I suppose the major difference between our families is a cultural one. I come from a Mediterranean tradition where my house is your house. If someone walks into your house, they can stay for days, weeks, months. That's the way you do it. Kate might have felt a bit strange when she visited my parents in Cyprus, but she once told me the one thing she's always dreamed of is having in-laws who would love her like their daughter. That's one thing my family will always do.

It's not the actual cultural difference between families that matters to me; it's manners. I know Kate can be abrupt – but she's very warm and she's always been so generous. But the whole issue with family has become a barrier for me and I don't feel as close to Kate's family as I'd like to sometimes. Maybe that's my own problem though. I tell Kate that she doesn't need to feel close to my family, but I can't see any reason why she wouldn't. They would do anything for her. My mum would sleep on the floor on cold tiles so that she would have a bed. She'd be treated like a queen in Cyprus. If we went to Australia, Kate would never have to lift a finger or pay a cent for anything. My family would never say anything to me, but I'm sure deep inside everyone has the same feeling. It eats away at me because my family are my best friends.

I remember a time when Kate would cook dinner and always serve up her own plate first. That's something I was brought up never to do. Serve your guests first and, if there's nothing left, so be it. But Kate has definitely changed a lot since we've been together. She's the most warm-hearted person I know. Plus, her family are great and I love them all.

Just to be clear, I am not saying that my ways are right and that other ways are wrong. Let's just say we are... different.

CHAPTER SIXTEEN
JUNIOR

IT'S TRUE I have a terrible memory for dates, but I'll never forget the day Junior was born: 13 June 2005, at 10.13am. It was the most incredible moment of my life.

I'd never felt it before and I didn't understand it, but I suppose it was the closest I've ever come to euphoria. I had my own sell-out concert at Wembley – my biggest dream – and I never experienced that feeling. It just doesn't compare to the way I felt when I held my son for the first time.

But I was the lucky one. Unfortunately for Kate, her pregnancy hadn't been plain sailing. Five weeks before she was due to give birth, the doctors identified a problem. There was a membrane above her cervix that had developed into a thick layer. Because of the way a baby is formed, it will naturally turn its head to engage. Our baby couldn't turn his head because of this membrane. Instead, he was lying horizontally, which made Kate's stomach look really bizarre and gave her a lot of pain. It also caused an imbalance in her hormones, causing her moods to swing erratically. It was certainly a tough time.

Dr Gibb initially told us the baby would become stronger and be able to break the membrane. But after a few weeks nothing had happened and the doctor said it had become an emergency. If Kate went into labour now, it could be fatal.

It was like a cruel joke after everything Kate had been through with her first pregnancy, with no father figure present to support her when her son was diagnosed with optic septic dysplasia. Now she did have someone by her side, serious problems were happening again. Sometimes I can't believe how much this poor woman has gone through. I know the whole world isn't about Kate and there are other women who have been through a lot and care for children with special needs, but Kate has never let herself be a victim. She's always been so positive about her situation. She's never asked for sympathy. And, because she's in the limelight, she has an opportunity to be a role model. People can learn from her experiences and realise that they aren't alone.

I was devastated when the doctors first broke the news to us. Please don't let this woman go through any more! I thought.

I had so desperately wanted everything to run smoothly for the birth of our first child. But sometimes these things are little taps on the shoulder to remind us that we shouldn't take anything for granted.

There was no turning back now. Within 24 hours the doctors would perform a Caesarean on Kate and our son would enter the world. I bought my parents plane tickets so that they could come over immediately and I booked them into the Cavendish Hotel. Then Kate and I drove to the Portland Hospital, where Claire stayed with us the night before the delivery.

Kate has an incredible fear of needles and was beginning to panic about having her epidural. In an attempt to calm her down, Claire acted out a role play, pretending to inject Kate in the back. Had anyone walked in, they would have thought we were all completely nuts. Not only is Claire a great manager, she is probably one of the most caring people I know.

I refused to leave Kate's side for a second. The night before the birth, I turned to her and asked, 'What shall I have as my final meal before I become a blood father?'

She looked at me and said, 'Well, what should I have for my final meal before I have a proper family.'

It was really sweet.

'Well, actually, we've been a proper family for nine months,' I said, smiling. So we ordered our usual pizza and went nuts!

A Caesarean hadn't been Kate's first choice, because she'd wanted a natural birth. In fact, when the doctors advised her to have a Caesarean she asked me if I minded. As if I had the right to tell her what to do! It was her body and her choice. All I've ever wanted – and all I'll ever want – is what's best for Kate. That night she was shaking and she couldn't sleep. She cried so much, because she was genuinely scared. It broke my heart because I was the lucky one who'd get to hold my baby in a few hours, whereas she had to go through all the pain. I gripped her hand the whole time. I didn't leave her sight. For the whole five days she was in hospital, not one second did I go outside except to make an announcement to the press. I didn't even go home to get changed. Being by her side meant such a lot to both of us.

On the morning of the birth, everyone arrived at 8am to give Kate their support. Only her mum and her friend Sally had been present for Harvey's birth. I think Kate found the number of people who were there quite overwhelming.

I'm an emotional person when it comes to one thing, and that's family. If I see a reunion on TV of parents and children who haven't seen each other for years, that can set me off. I don't cry at romantic movies, but when it's about families I do. In the hours leading up to Junior's birth, I was an emotional wreck.

The nurses arrived to take Kate downstairs for her epidural. Mum and Dad gave me a kiss and said, 'Look after her.' Her mum came down in the lift with us, but she wasn't allowed in the theatre. I'm sure that was very hard for Amy, because she's been through so much with Kate. I admire her for letting me do my thing. Kate and Amy were crying and that set me off, because again it was family.

We went into the theatre and Kate started to panic about the needles. I held her hand, told her to close her eyes and promised I'd count her down. I decided I would only start counting after they'd actually put the needle in so that it would be over before she even realised what was going on.

The nurses were rubbing her back and I saw the doctor about to put the needle in.

'When's it going to happen?' Kate asked, trembling.

'Don't worry, I'll count you down,' I said and started to count. 'Ten, nine...' The needle had gone in. 'Eight...'

By the time I got to one, I said, 'It's done.'

I was overcome by such a strange feeling, knowing that soon I'd be holding our son, my first child, in my arms. By now, Kate was surrounded by doctors. The theatre felt strangely peaceful. It was almost like an eerie kind of heavenly feeling. There are so many bright lights and the outside world is completely shut out.

The doctors put a screen up above Kate's belly button. I stood near the middle of the screen, so I could see everything. I was starting to feel nervous, but I didn't want Kate to see. The doctors were starting to cut her and I was already feeling overpowered by emotion. My poor girl, why are they hurting you? I thought. A doctor grabbed each side of her stomach and literally ripped her open. I could see blood everywhere. It was the most horrific thing I've ever witnessed. Seeing that has given me a respect for Kate beyond comparison.

I saw her looking around while she was open, then all of the sudden I could hear a song in the background. I couldn't believe my ears. It was our song, 'A Whole New World'.

'It's our song!' smiled Kate.

It was a total coincidence.

By now, I was feeling extremely emotional.

'Your baby's about to arrive,' said the doctor. Even now when I think about it I have goosebumps. Kate's waters burst as the song was approaching the chorus and all of a sudden I could see the head of our son. That was it. I was gone. Hysterical. Here I was, witnessing the arrival of the greatest gift that Jehovah could give me – my son.

'That's our baby!' said Kate as the doctor lifted him above the screen.

Through tear-soaked eyes, I kept looking between Kate and our baby. At that moment I felt I'd been given the greatest gift in the world. I kept saying to Kate, 'I love you so much.' I don't think anything in the world can ever compare with that feeling. It was as if I'd seen heaven for the first time.

The doctors handed the baby to me. As incredible as that was, they really should have given him to Kate first. I took him over to the nurse because she needed to clean him up. I'm sad to say it, but there was a 30-minute wait before Kate even held him. I was running back and forth between Kate and the baby. Kate was dazed and confused and didn't know what was going on. I brought the baby to her and said, 'This is your son!'

'Please, Pete,' she said. 'I'm going to be sick. I can't look at you or the baby.'

It must have been at that moment that the rejection first started. Her behaviour wasn't normal. A mother would hold the baby and cry, but she didn't want to hold the baby. At the time I didn't notice anything, because I was too emotional. It was a completely selfish act at that moment. I wasn't considering Kate's feelings.

We went upstairs and, as soon as the lift door opened, I saw my parents and I burst into tears.

'Mum, Dad – we did it!' I shouted.

My mum started crying and then my dad started crying, which he never does – never! On our documentary he said he never thought he'd actually get so emotional.

'I can't do this on film,' he said, then walked out.

I knew then that he understood the love I was feeling. It probably took him back 50-odd years to when it first happened to him. Kate's mum was in tears as well. The only person unsure of what was going on was Kate. I was really happy that my brother Michael could be with us, because he had always been there from the beginning. He bought us our first pregnancy test and he was the first person to know.

When everyone left, I was alone with Kate and Junior. I couldn't stop staring at Junior and I kept kissing them both. But Kate was still feeling ill and she needed a lot of rest. That night we fell asleep in each other's arms. I was lying next to Kate on a single hospital bed. When I came upstairs the next day, Claire told me I had to go outside and make a press announcement. This is so bizarre, I thought. Where have I arrived at in the last few years that I've got to come out and talk to the world about my wife and son? It was too strange. I was so nervous. There were photographers everywhere. I told them, 'Unfortunately for Kate – but fortunately for me – he's my spitting image. I'm ecstatic.' For the first time in my life I'd achieved a success that I could be truly proud of. It was something that no one could ever take away from me.

CHAPTER SEVENTEEN

BABY BLUES

ONCE THE COMMOTION had subsided and my feet had finally touched the ground, I noticed there was definitely something wrong with Kate. She was almost letting me get on with looking after Junior. She didn't seem to be connecting with our new son. I didn't want to say anything, because I thought maybe she was just really tired. But it didn't seem normal.

This continued for a long, long time. It was only six months after the birth that Kate finally admitted to me there was a problem. To be honest, I'd known from day one. I just couldn't understand why she didn't want to hold Junior herself but didn't want anyone else to touch him either. Whenever she woke up in the morning or came in from work, she would instinctively go straight to Harvey. It almost felt as if Junior didn't exist to Kate – which I couldn't understand as I loved him so very much.

Looking back, I was probably partly to blame. When

Kate fell pregnant, one of her greatest fears was that I'd love the new child more than Harvey. It became an added stress. I gave my word that I would be with her throughout the pregnancy and would take care of the baby as much as I could, so that she could concentrate on looking after Harvey. I was determined to make sure Junior wasn't a burden to her. With hindsight, I shouldn't have interfered. At the time, I thought I was doing the right thing; that the last thing she needed was another child screaming in her ear.

It was hurting me so much, as my family means everything to me, but still I was afraid to push the issue. Strangely enough, a week before Junior's birth, the topic of post-natal depression had come up in conversation.

'Oh, that would be just my luck if I rejected the baby,' joked Kate. So part of me thought it was playing on her mind. But her fears had actually come true.

I can't believe Kate's bad luck sometimes. Here's a woman who has every bit of success in her career, but then in other areas she seems to be so unfortunate. It's almost as if she's been blessed and cursed at the same time, though I think her blessings outweigh the bad a million times over. One thing I admire so much about Kate is that she doesn't let Harvey's disability stop her from doing anything. She's a strong woman and that's why people love her. That's why I love her.

My parents stayed with us for three days. I have to admit it was a difficult time. To their credit, they were only trying to help out and as a family we've never known any other way. When cousins have had babies, everyone has looked after them.

'How long are you staying here for?' Amy said to my parents. 'My daughter really needs to be left alone.'

Kate never told me she wanted my family to stay in a hotel and I had asked her. My parents did nothing but show love. They were there to cook, to help, to clean the place, to make sure Kate was comfortable. She obviously wanted to be left alone – probably even by me – but, unless she told me, how was I supposed to know? I thought it was really considerate of my parents. They didn't come to be entertained.

This is the sort of thing I find hard to understand with Kate. My family are my life, and that includes Kate, Junior and Harvey. It's all about love. My house is open. If Kate has a problem with that, then she should tell me and we can talk about it. But she was the one who said, tell your parents to come over, I'm having the baby. Then she didn't want anyone around. I know her behaviour was in part due to the hormonal changes she was going through with the pregnancy.

Her depression and mood swings caused a lot of problems. A distance developed between us and it was something I hadn't encountered before. But I wanted to stick by her, because I knew it was a phase. I understood that plenty of other women had been through similar traumas.

We argued a lot during that period. I think the lowest point for me was when I read excerpts from her book and I realised what she had been feeling. I felt so hurt that she hadn't sat down and told me. She told the world and not me. It really, really hurt me. I was that hurt, I really felt that I wanted some time out on my own. But I considered the kids.

I admit my insistence on choosing Junior's name didn't really help matters. The Greek tradition is – and it's a respect thing – that the first boy in the family is named after the bride or groom's father. We had already reached an agreement to call our baby Daniel, because it was her brother's name and my brother's name. Then his middle name could be Savva – the Greek word for Sabbath – which is my dad's name.

I went to Cyprus and told my parents we'd come up with a great name, but I could see the pained look on Dad's face.

'Aren't you going to name him after your father?' Mum asked me.

'No,' I said.

Then I went away and thought about it. Maybe they were right. So I came back but, instead of discussing it with Kate, I said to her, I think we should call him Savva. It was a bit mean of me, because we'd already decided on his name.

Kate wasn't having it and we argued a lot.

'I don't like the name Savva,' she screamed, which really offended me.

Eventually we came to a compromise. Kate suggested Junior and I couldn't believe it because it was one of my favourite names as a kid. We kept his middle name as Savva, so he became Junior Savva, which means he's a mini version of my dad. That way, it kept everything sweet. Although I admit it was selfish of me to make a decision without consulting Kate, I guess I was torn about what to do. But I can't just do what makes me happy. This is 2006 and things don't always go according to tradition.

Kate was going through a lot of depression and no one in the outside world knew what was happening. It was really frustrating me, because I knew everything but I couldn't talk to anyone about it. Nobody. I didn't want anyone to know. Kate was agitated, didn't want to see anybody and would sometimes lock herself in her room. I don't know how we got through it.

Kate wanted my mum and dad to know what she was going through and how she'd rejected the baby. Things were not looking good and she decided to see the doctor.

I said to her, 'I will stick by you 100 per cent, provided you want to help yourself. If I know you want to help yourself and go to see the doctor, then I'll know you're making an effort and I'll stick by you through it. But, if you don't want to and you can't be bothered and you'd rather get your hair and nails done, then this is going to drive me away. I can't do this.' I said this to Kate, because I remembered that, when I had suffered from depression, I'd needed to help myself or I would not have got through it.

She went to the doctor and certain things were discussed. It wasn't the easiest of times and I'd be lying if I said our relationship was absolute bliss then. There are low points and we do argue, but we have learned to talk everything through. What holds us together through these kinds of times is our love for each other. It enables us to weather so many storms. I've invested so much in Kate – as I know she has in me – and we won't give up on each other, there is just too much love between us.

Yes, her sex drive came back over time, but not dramatically. I've proved to her that I can go without sex. It's not the problem. The problem is that, apart from that, I need some sort of comfort and understanding. You can be doing all these photo shoots and everything looks so glossy, but behind the scenes there's so much going on. Sometimes we'd be on TV doing some great interviews and I'd have this look on my face that I wanted to cry for help. But I couldn't. Yes, Kate was going through the pain. She was in the eye of the storm, but I was being hit by all the debris. It was hitting me left, right and centre. Yes, she needs help, but I also need help. I wanted so much to ask for help. I needed advice. Then I'd fight through it.

Our relationship has been an interesting one, to say the least. But Kate knows in her heart that, financially, I could stand on my own two feet for the rest of my life. It's not about that. She knows me now. I want this relationship to work, because I want us to be together and I love her with all my heart.

Sometimes it was starting to split at the seams, but we had this solid backbone and I think that's why it stayed pretty strong. But it has been tough. Her insecurities grew during this period and she was extremely jealous of any girls who even looked at me. Whenever we went out I'd always have to keep my eyes on the ground. Yes, I was a little sexually frustrated, but I wasn't about to go and cheat on her. I needed to reassure her that my commitment was solid. I didn't want to go out. I felt I was becoming really enclosed. That's why I need to constantly see my family. I need to see my brothers, my sister and my parents – that's my outlet. If Kate or anyone else doesn't understand that, that's their problem, I'm afraid. I don't care. That's me.

That's not bad. If I needed to go out and get pissed with my mates every night, then I'd understand why it was a problem. But all I'm asking for is my family. And that's nothing but love.

Kate sometimes worries that I might love Junior more than Harvey. Not true. Yes, Junior's my blood and of course the bond between us is special. I can see where she's coming from, but Harvey is my special boy. Sometimes, she seems to think my mum might love Junior more than Harvey. It's simply not true. It's just a different kind of love.

I find remarks like that unfair because, when her mum used to come over in the morning to pick up Harvey, she'd walk in and go straight to Harvey. She has always been with Harvey from the beginning. But I've never complained. I don't care about saying it because it's the truth. If it was a lie, it would be wrong. She opened up a can of worms in her book, so I've got to heal some wounds.

Since she went to see the doctor, Kate has improved a lot with Junior. She took a month off work to sort out her problems. Gradually I noticed little things happening. I'd see that she wanted to bath and feed him and sometimes I'd go upstairs and they'd be asleep in the same bed and she'd be cuddled up to him. That kind of thing, which I thought would be normal, wasn't happening for the first six months. Seeing those changes take place has been amazing – to the point where I've said, 'Oh, babe, I can't be bothered bathing them tonight. Can you do it?' I do it partly because I want her to really bond with Junior and partly because it was so intense for me for the first six months. She instinctively went to Harvey first and I instinctively went to Junior, because that's how it was for the first six months. But balance started to return after Christmas.

Fortunately, our two sons don't argue nearly as much as their parents! Whenever another baby comes into the house Harvey usually goes nuts, but with Junior he must have sensed something. We'd often go upstairs and find Harvey sitting next to Junior's cot, just staring at him. Nowadays when Harvey comes downstairs, the first thing he says is "unior'. But don't let me paint too pretty a picture – he still gives him a wallop sometimes.

In those difficult times, what kept me here is the kids, my love for Kate and the fact I want to support her. I came out of the jungle and I had the world at my feet. It could have gone to my head but I chose to make a family.

CHAPTER EIGHTEEN
K AND P

ONCE I'D PROPOSED to Kate she was very keen for the wedding to take place soon afterwards, whereas I had in mind that we'd be engaged for a couple of years. That would give us time to get to know each other properly. But Kate did make a valid point. 'If you believe I'm the one, why wait?' she complained. 'I know you're the one!'

As much as I believed in my heart that I was going to marry her, I did still think we should wait a couple of years. But she fell pregnant and that was another factor for me. I believe Kate needed to know that this wasn't just for the moment, but was going to be for real. She needed that final commitment. Funnily enough, I never liked her calling me her 'boyfriend' anyway. I hate that word because it sounds so temporary. 'Fiancé' is nice but 'husband' is even better!

Claire said it would be impossible to get married so quickly and have such a big do, but Kate didn't want to wait. What with her post-natal depression, there was so much tension in the household. Perhaps it wasn't the right time. But then an opportunity came up for 10 September. If this is meant to work, I thought, it will. Another year won't change that. We're having a child together and we're both bringing up Harvey. We love our life and each other. Let's do it.

I wanted to leave all the planning to Kate. She had this picture of a wedding that was all glitz and glam – tacky to some but I'd say it was more fairy-tale. We were out shopping in Toys R Us for the kids one day and Kate dragged me to an aisle full of Barbie dolls.

'This is what I want our wedding to look like!' she screamed, reaching for a Barbie and Ken horse and carriage set. We bought the toy and presented it to Claire.

'This is what we're after,' we told her. So Claire went about putting plans in place.

I wanted Kate to pick it all but she insisted I be part of the preparations. Emma, our wedding planner, was great. She made all our dreams come true. We left nothing out.

As the wedding drew near, Harvey was in and out of hospital. At one point the doctors said they'd need him to stay in for at least six weeks. It was touch and go whether he'd actually make the ceremony. We cancelled a lot of our meetings and work in London and stayed in hotels overnight. For weeks, Kate would stay with Harvey one night and I'd stay the next. We visited him as much as we could. We didn't want to go home without Harvey. Once again, Amy was brilliant and devoted a lot of her time to Harvey and us.

In the middle of all this we were trying to plan a

wedding. Sometimes we'd even have a meeting downstairs in the hospital canteen. There were moments when we'd be excited about the wedding, then suddenly we'd feel down. If Harvey can't be there, we thought, then what's the point? Let's delay it. But there was always the worry that he might just end up in hospital again. It was a tough time. Kate was still suffering from post-natal depression. The stress was becoming incredible and we were having the worst arguments.

I wanted there to be a lot of ivory and a lot more masculine colours. I didn't want it to be all pink, for goodness sake! Other than that, I agreed with most of what was said. I took control of the entertainment side of things as that was my realm. Emma and I chose Brazilian drummers and quartets. I've seen shows like Cirque du Soleil in Vegas and I've done tours of my own where we've used acrobats, so I knew what I was looking for. As for the flowers and decorations, that was a mystery to me. It would have driven me nuts.

I looked at so many different vocalists. Originally, I wanted the London Gospel Choir. One thing was for certain: I didn't want the traditional wedding song. We decided on 'I Have Nothing (If I Don't Have You)' by Whitney Houston. I had this vision in my mind in which everyone would walk down the aisle in time to different sections of the song. The bridesmaids, Harvey, Kate – each party would walk down to a certain lyric. As soon as they sing the first words of the chorus, 'Don't make me close', Katie appears. It happened exactly like that. I knew each line, each moment it should happen.

Despite my strong cultural ties, I insisted on very few Greek traditions at our wedding. For a start, I had to consider that not everyone coming was Greek! But I desperately wanted some Greek music to be played for our guests. 'I don't see the point,' Kate complained, digging her heels in. 'People who aren't Greek won't understand any of it!'

'But more than half the guests will be Greek!' I protested.

'I don't think anyone will understand it,' she repeated.

'No, anyone who's not cultured won't understand it,' I spat back.

We argued about it and I got really shitty because she was being so narrow-minded.

'I have a say in this wedding as well,' I insisted. 'I'm getting married too.'

But then a week before the wedding Kate and I went out to Cyprus for Mum and Dad's fiftieth wedding anniversary. During the celebration my brother Chris got up and played for everyone. Chris is multi-talented and plays 11 instruments, some Greek and some English. People were getting up on the tables and dancing. Kate turned around, clearly impressed, and said, 'Oh my God, we need to have this at our wedding!'

I could have killed her.

So we booked Chris for an hour-long set and I even got up and did some Greek dancing: the zembekiko, a very slow, rhythmic and passionate dance. Guys will dance together first and then girls get up and do the same. My best friend George agreed to join me on stage and we received a massive round of applause.

Kate's stubbornness does bug me. She'll have something in her mind and that's it! I get a bit upset because I want her to be more open-minded and to understand things. I love experiencing and understanding different cultures. To me that's the real beauty of the world. Having said that, we are seeing a lot of the world together at the moment!

I asked Bill Forman, who had done such a wonderful job of Kate's engagement ring, to design her wedding ring as well. I had an idea of what I wanted. She'd already asked for something massive. I also had my heart set on pink diamonds, which are quite rare. We created a dome of 35 princess-cut diamonds, with pink diamonds encrusted in rose gold. I knew it would cost a fortune, but I didn't care because this was the symbol of my love and this would be a special moment for us to treasure for ever. Bill said it would take three months to make the ring I wanted. Little did I know that Kate had contacted him and said, 'I don't know what you're designing for me, but I want you to design something for Pete that will match mine – but more of a masculine version.'

For my groomsmen I had platinum rings made with 'Katie and Peter September 05' engraved on them. For her bridesmaids Kate had earrings made with smaller versions of the diamonds on our rings. Both our mums were given white gold diamond rings, again with princess-cut diamonds. I thought those were really special gifts. We didn't get anything for our dads, because they don't like jewellery or fuss.

My only other area of expertise in the wedding planning was the food. Surprise, surprise! We had the most amazing food-tasting sessions at our house. Two different companies came over and spent the day giving us a taste of every canapé, every starter and every main course on offer. It was incredible. Whereas everyone else would nibble at tiny bits, I ate everything. I cleaned up and I could have eaten enough for 12 people that day.

Four weeks later we had another tasting. I could quite get used to these. They set everything up in the kitchen and cooked for us, but we weren't allowed in. We had a wedding when each of the companies came round! Both companies were so good we didn't know which to choose. We invited Kate's mum Amy and Claire to join us. Everyone else kept complaining they couldn't taste another bit of food, but I couldn't get enough.

The canapés were really unique and amazing; you'd have roast lamb, roast potatoes and Yorkshire puddings all on the size of a teaspoon. Then there were cheeseburgers the size of a 5p coin. You could have eaten the canapés and been full. We chose only one main dish. I wanted three – lamb, chicken and fish. But everyone agreed on one chicken and one vegetarian. For a starter we had lobster with beautiful sauces, and it was really elegantly presented. For dessert they came up with a heart-shaped cake full of a custard-type sauce. On top were the letters K and P with an arrow going through the heart.

True to form, we pulled out all the stops for our wedding cake as well. It was made by a company called Choccywoccydoodah, who kindly donated it to us. We were told it was going to be five feet high and larger than life. When we saw it, Kate and I looked at each other and said,

'Oh, is that it?' It was a lot smaller than we'd imagined. But it was still an incredible-looking cake. The worst thing was, not only did neither of us try a piece of that cake, but we had a 'Cakegate' scandal at the end of the night when somebody stole it! The very next day we asked for the cake and were informed that the waiters had been told to throw it away, even though it was only a quarter eaten. Kate and I were really disappointed, because we'd planned on saving the little figures on top.

Both my suit and Kate's dress were designed by Isabell Kristensen. I had three fittings in total – two in London at Isabell's shop and one in Monaco. We flew over just to have a fitting. That was quite decadent. The suit was actually taken in twice between fittings, which I was really happy about, because I was scared I had put on weight.

I wasn't allowed to see Kate's dress but she was allowed to see my suit, which I thought was a bit mean. The suit was so heavy it felt like armour. I can't imagine how Kate must have felt in her dress. Claire did warn her, 'You won't be comfortable on the night. It's going to feel really heavy. I'm just telling you, Kate, as I know what you will be like on the day.'

But Kate insisted on it. At midnight she changed into her tutu, but the tiara was so heavy she couldn't take it any more. She lasted until 3am.

We still have the dress and the suit and we're waiting to display them somewhere. They were such a one-off and it seems a waste to leave them hanging in a safe, collecting dust. My suit, which cost a fortune to make, was covered in Swarovski crystals and ivory. We'd like to keep them in a museum, not just because they were our wedding clothes, but because they are truly beautiful pieces.

Money was never a real worry, because I wanted Kate to have everything she'd ever wanted. But, with a wedding like that, where's the limit? When we got to a million we stopped. We each paid half and neither of us had to ask our parents, which made us very proud. We were so honoured to bring them to the wedding we made. But we knew that, without our deal with *OK!* and the blessing of Richard Desmond, we couldn't have put on such a lavish event. Richard and his wife Janet have become great friends of ours.

Before I met Kate I'd done a couple of glossy magazines, but Kate had already done some work with *OK!*. Soon after we got together in the jungle, they became interested in us as a couple. They approached us about doing an interview and they had such a great response from readers that they set up a contract. It's become an unbelievable source of income and security for me, and for both parties I believe it's been a beneficial deal both ways.

OK! were involved very heavily in our wedding arrangements. We didn't want to try to deny our relationship or keep it hidden from the public. Everyone saw our love blossom in the jungle, so why were we going to knock back a deal that would help pay for part of our wedding and help the world share in our dream? People pay big bucks to have photos done at their wedding and we were lucky enough to be paid to have photographs at ours. *OK!* have been the greatest. We know now that there is one magazine you can take for gospel; a lot of things get printed in other publications that are speculation. Richard

Desmond is such a nice man and I wanted to thank him properly at our wedding. The magazine is a big part of my life now. They've helped put me back on my feet in this country and in Europe.

I would be foolish to complain about the media involvement in our lives. After all, we got to tell our story. When the time comes that Kate and I want to be on our own, we'll stop doing it. I admit that the TV crews can be a bit intrusive. But when we were initially approached with the idea of making a documentary, I always said we should just have cameras all over the house. I wanted it to be real, even if we do behave like idiots sometimes! That's what makes it good viewing. I don't always watch our show. I have to be in the right mood. There are things that are said and done that I don't want to hear again and I definitely don't want to see myself the way I've looked in some of those programmes. But Kate and I have never put on an act. We're very honest people and we are exactly as you find us. That's why it works – it's real and not just an overproduced staged production.

Getting married is a really draining experience, and we were arguing a lot. The guest list was a real problem because the venue for the wedding ceremony would only hold 108 people. I come from a very large Greek family. If I were to invite my aunts, uncles and first cousins alone, there would be 141 guests. Contrary to many newspaper reports, we weren't obliged to invite a certain number of celebrities. I didn't want to bring people I didn't know. The only person I wanted to invite whom I didn't know was George Michael, because he's been a massive inspiration to me.

I met him once a long time ago and he was the only person that I didn't know what to say to. I am convinced he thought I was an arrogant little shit or a snob. As for everyone else, if I don't know them I don't care. The only celebrities I really wanted to invite were my jungle friends. The whole issue of the guest list was quite a pressure.

But all the people on our list were there for a reason. We invited Boy George, because he and Kate are friends. Paul Gascoigne and Kate had met loads of times and he was one of the only ones who had believed in her from the beginning. Vanessa Feltz has always been supportive and honest about Kate and I.

The lead-up to the wedding was stressful. Whether we were choosing colour schemes or dealing with Kate's post-natal depression, it all became a bit too much! I really thought at one point, Why the f**k am I getting married? I'm trapped in a shell. I don't know where I'm going or what I'm doing. Those months between Junior being born and us getting married were tough for Kate and I. Then I remembered how I felt when I first met Kate. When I first met Harvey. I thought of Junior and the love we have between the four of us. We're our own fantastic four.

In the end I didn't have a stag do. That was another thing I sacrificed for Kate. She had a hen do at a health farm, but it was arranged through our management for a magazine. She desperately begged me not to have a stag do. She didn't trust me 100 per cent. She couldn't believe that there wouldn't be a stripper or that I wouldn't get up to something.

'If you do have a stag do, it's your choice,' she said. I was waiting for a 'but'. 'But if anyone comes out with a story we won't get married – even if it's not true.'

I wasn't prepared to take that risk, so I passed up a stag do. It was hard, because all my friends wanted to throw one. Instead, I went to Cyprus for a few days to spend some time with my family. I wanted Kate to come with me, but she was too busy working. But I figured a short break would give me some time to check on our new house. Plus I wanted to take Junior to see Mum and Dad as I hoped that might help ease the pressure on Kate.

Totally unbeknown to me, she was fuming. She hated the fact that I'd gone and taken Junior with me. But, once again, how was I supposed to know unless she told me? She said it was fine. I can't read her mind. In any other family, if a father wants to take his son to see his parents, that's normal. Sometimes I don't know what world she comes from! I waved it off as post-natal depression. I hoped I was right.

Highclere Castle, the venue we finally chose for our wedding, was a truly magnificent setting for what would be the second most memorable day of my life. Because of our security requirements, Claire faced so many problems in finding a suitable venue and ended up searching the whole country. The night before the wedding, Kate and I stayed in separate rooms. She was sharing a room with Sarah from Girls Aloud and Michelle Heaton. I had my best man, George, my mate Reno and my brothers Chris and Michael. It was really good fun. I stayed up until 4am because I was so excited. The boys and I went downstairs with Sarah and Michelle for a few drinks. We were creeping around the castle trying to break into forbidden rooms. There was one

'Sacred Room' which contained a desk once used by Napoleon. We were all behaving like kids, but it felt like my chance to let my hair down.

I slept for just three or four hours that night. After all Kate and I had been through, from our humble start in the jungle, I couldn't believe we were actually getting married.

Unlike Kate, it didn't take me long to get ready. Gary Cockerill, who has been Kate's make-up artist from the start, agreed to do the make-up for all of us. He's great, because he knows how to groom men and women alike.

'Come on, Gary, make me look beautiful for today!' I joked.

Isabell Kristensen flew in especially from Monaco on the day to help me with my suit.

Nick Malenko and Royston Blythe were doing our hair. I decided to have extensions put in for the day, because I was going for a princely look. I wanted it to be long and pushed back, so that it was timeless and classic.

These days I'm not so embarrassed about male grooming and beauty treatments. Funnily enough, I actually care less about my image now. I had some Botox injections before the wedding, but I wasn't afraid to admit it. Back in 1997 I even had a nose job. Towards the end, when I was getting paranoid, I always thought that my nose looked really big. Back then it was taboo to have corrective surgery. I asked Claire and we went to an American doctor who'd done Toni Braxton's nose. We even had a secret name for the whole operation, always referring to my nose as 'code orange'. I had the operation right before we filmed the 'All About Us' video.

The minute I'd had it done, my confidence rocketed. It was

reported in the press, but I denied it because back then I denied things. Now I don't care. That's one thing Kate has taught me. She always says, 'Just admit it and tell people the truth and that way they can't slate you for anything.'

These days I care less about my image, but I wouldn't rule out cosmetic surgery completely! I would like to grow old gracefully, but I'm not going to grow old gracefully if my wife's going to look like she's 20 years old when she's 60!

As the day approached, there was so much fuss around Kate, whereas there were times when I was left on my own in my room. My brothers would be coming in and out and I'd be thinking, I'm glad I'm actually invited to the wedding! I almost felt like an outsider. I was the one behind the scenes. When everyone would leave the room I would stay behind, thinking, This is where it will all happen in half an hour.

Everyone in the world saw Kate arrive in her magical carriage; everyone except me. I was in the bathroom having a cigarette to calm my nerves. I could hear the helicopters, but I wasn't allowed to peek out unless a photo was taken. I was hearing what everyone else was seeing. I could picture Kate arriving in the carriage and I could hear the people cheering. I could hear the trumpeters playing. I was so excited.

As I stood at the altar I knew I was going to burst out crying. I walked into the room and I remember Vanessa Feltz winking at me as if to say, Good on you. I'm proud of you. All my cousins were there. I remember seeing all their faces.

'Sorry, I can't talk to anyone. I'm a bit nervous,' I said, my hands trembling, beads of sweat starting to appear on my brow. I remember that feeling, this is the biggest step in my life. I was nervous, anxious but happy. My body stiffened, waiting for that moment.

I'd never seen Kate's dress before, but I'd heard it was amazing and contained 800 sheets of Swarovski crystals. I thought to myself, Oh my God, am I actually going to be able to hold this woman? Will I even be in the wedding photos? All of a sudden I heard everyone sit down. I froze, my eyes fixed ahead of me. The gospel singer stepped forward and broke into 'I Have Nothing'. My heart started beating fast. This is it, I thought.

Everything went to plan. We had rehearsed the ceremony the previous night and I knew exactly when everyone would be walking down the aisle. As Harvey walked down, I turned around and saw him. Only days before, he'd been in hospital and we weren't sure if he would make the wedding. That was the moment when I realised I couldn't hold back my tears any longer. People might think I lost it because I saw Kate in her dress but there was a lot about Harvey walking down that aisle that touched me. His being there was the absolute icing on the cake.

Then I heard the singer hit the high note and everyone gasped, so I knew Kate had appeared. Everyone except me saw her, but I didn't want to turn round because I knew I'd lose it. I had tears in my eyes. When she was three-quarters of the way down the aisle, I saw her and that was it. I was gone. She looked so beautiful. I looked at her and saw her eyes well up and, knowing that she's not a girl who normally cries unless she is really hurt, this truly touched me. I told her she looked unbelievable.

The lady conducting the ceremony asked us to speak and

I couldn't believe how difficult it was to repeat a few simple words. At that moment I was in a completely different world. This is it. I was getting married. In terms of how big a step I was taking, I could only compare it to having a sex change or a complete surgical makeover, not that I've had either... yet (just joking!). What I mean is that, from that second on, you know your life has changed for ever. I stumbled through my vows and, before I knew it, it was over.

We did ask for a number of vows to be changed. For instance, we were keen to include the word 'respect'. None of Kate's family is religious and I didn't want to impose my own beliefs on anyone. For that reason we had opted for a civil wedding. Because certain words like 'Jesus' aren't permitted to be used, we had to choose our songs quite carefully. We also chose to include the words 'loyalty' and 'faithfulness' – we didn't want any excuse. Where the vows read, 'Till death do us part,' I added, 'I promise to be faithful.'

The one thing that stuck in my mind was when they said, 'Can we have the rings, please?' As George passed me the ring, I said to Kate, 'You wait till you see this!' As I put it on her finger, everyone gasped. I mean, it was huge. She couldn't even close her finger properly. But Kate, in her true style, said, 'You ain't seen yours yet!' And here's me expecting her to burst into tears! She was right. Mine was like a knuckleduster. Claire, Neville and I call it 'The Fridge'!

'You can kiss the bride,' I was told and all I remember thinking was how hot it was in there. Why would she want to kiss me now? We couldn't have any of the fans switched on in case it interfered with the TV crew's recording equipment.

I enjoyed every minute of the wedding, but Kate didn't like a certain photographer that *OK!* had requested to take our pictures, plus she is used to our own team now. And when she gets a bee in her bonnet... She already had the hump before he even started to take photos, so every photo was one too many. But I didn't want to waste a second of this beautiful day. In fact, I didn't think we took enough photos. I would have loved more of all the families together.

My best man George gave a speech half in English and half in Greek. Just before he was due to start he had a last-minute panic and said he couldn't do it. But he went from not wanting to say anything to giving a marathon speech. 'This is not just about you, son, it's about us,' he said. Thanks, Georgie, it was an incredible speech.

Katie's stepdad, Paul, also did a speech. He had been just as nervous as George, and had practised it over and over again in front of the family and Claire, so that he would be word perfect on the day. And he was – it was a wonderful speech. My mate Reno was too nervous to give a speech.

My only real regret of the day was that I didn't get to see all the entertainment we'd so carefully planned. We were determined there would never be a moment when people were bored. Every half an hour there had to be a complete change of atmosphere. A group of Brazilian drummers led our guests outside into the grounds of the castle. We ran a projection on the outside wall, the size of the whole castle, with footage of me and Kate meeting in the jungle. Then there were images of us as kids, stuff that people had never seen before. It was a real surprise for our parents!

One other highlight of the night was a group of singing waiters. At first no one knew they were actually part of the entertainment. One waiter came out of the kitchen and caused a massive scene by interrupting the proceedings. Our guests were just about to start eating dinner.

'I'm really sorry, but one of the other waiters has dared me to come out and sing for Peter and Katie,' he announced to everyone.

Only Kate and I knew what was really going on.

'What the hell's goin' on?' I said, throwing my napkin on the floor and pretending to lose my temper. 'Shall we get security?'

All of a sudden he burst into a terrible song. It was so cringe-worthy! Another girl rushed out from the kitchen and screamed, 'Get back in here!'

Then she said, 'I'm so sorry.'

All of a sudden the waiter with the crappy voice came out with an incredible operatic voice. All the other waiters joined in and gave a great performance.

Around 3am Kate started to complain she felt tired and wanted to go to bed. This was probably the first night in years that I felt I could go on all night. I'd had a few but I wasn't drunk. I was simply in such a happy state. But Kate wasn't happy and it played on my mind. I was going to take her upstairs and then come back down to be with my guests. But as I was walking her up I thought, You can't do that! It's your wife! You should stay with her, it's your wedding night. I did feel the night was cut way too short, but I was happy to be with my new wife. Kate's mum and her stepdad, Paul, came into the room and we all had crisp sandwiches in bed.

I didn't mind. It was fun. Had it been the other way round, I don't know whether Kate would have agreed or not.

We had a wedding breakfast the next day and I was so happy, excited... and relieved it was all over. The papers were out and we read all the news stories. We even sat down and had a chat with the lord and lady of the manor! I was most concerned about our guests. Kate and I did argue a little bit because she was slightly less concerned about the welfare of our guests, but it was very important to me. I had a lot of guests over from Cyprus who didn't even speak English and I didn't want to forget about them just because I wanted to be happy. I found that selfish. But, once I knew they were OK, I was happy. Sometimes Kate falls into this selfish behaviour, but she does genuinely care and every day I see her radiating more warmth and love. When I look back, I can see how much more settled we are now than we were then.

We went on our honeymoon two weeks later, once we knew Harvey was completely in the clear. If he hadn't been able to come with us, we'd have cancelled the honeymoon. After all, we'd done things the other way round and had children before getting married, so it was only fair that they should share in our experience. The second problem was that Junior didn't have a passport. The law had just changed and all babies were now required to have their own documents. What should have been a blissful holiday was rapidly becoming a complete headache.

On the way to the airport Kate felt harassed and stressed. Now we have great help with our kids, we're a lot more in control. We have two nannies who provide 24-hour cover whenever we need them. Before, we were doing everything ourselves and it was very tiring.

We'd already struck up a deal with *OK!* and the makers of our TV series to film part of our honeymoon. Because of the work element to the trip, I decided to dub it the 'moneymoon'. It was agreed that the magazine and TV crews would stay with us for the first five days and then we'd have a week or two to ourselves. It was quite full-on, because we had Claire, our stylist Kerry-Ann, Shauna, who was filming, Gary and Phil and Kate's mum with us.

But it was really good and we felt a bit gutted when they all left. We loved their company. Work sometimes doesn't feel like work as we are all good friends.

The Maldives is the best place in the whole world. Neither of us had ever been there before. We stayed in a villa on the water, the Hilton in Rangali Island, with a long catwalk that extended out into the sea. It's only possible to reach the islands by sea plane and Claire made sure no snooping photographers could access our secret hideaway. Our villa was stunning. It costs £2,500 a night and only attracts the most exclusive guests. The floor in the living room was completely made of glass and we would spend hours watching the fish swim below. Outside, a veranda dipped into the water. We even had a 24-hour butler. Not a soul could see us and we enjoyed complete privacy, which is great because we like to sunbathe naked. We spent the days fishing, snorkelling and sunbathing. The villa provides these great beauty treatments where the husband and wife can lie next to each other, both staring into the ocean through a glass floor.

The Maldives has become our favourite holiday destination because we always feel so comfortable. Especially that one particular villa! If it was possible, we'd book it up every year!

Every day was packed with activity. We made full use of the water sports available on the island. I'm a jet-skiing freak and I love doing weird tricks and spinning, even though I know it's really dangerous. Kate was very scared of the jet ski because she'd never been on one before, but I persuaded her to have a go. One minute she'd be screaming and the next she'd calm down.

Several of the local fishing boats arranged special fishing trips for us. Whatever we caught, they'd take back to the mainland and cook for us. We had some great times with the crews. But there's one particular trip that I'll never forget. That morning I promised Kate I'd catch us something fantastic for dinner. But I ended up with a lot more than I bargained for. Traditionally, they don't use fishing rods in the Maldives, just lines. You have to be a man and wind your catch in by hand, with no gloves or aids. And they catch some big fish out there! Everyone on the trip was catching little babies.

'I'm gonna catch a massive one, I'm gonna catch a massive one!' I boasted to Kate.

Within seconds I felt a strong force tugging at my hand. The line slipped and wrapped around three of my fingers. I thought it was going to shred my skin. I've never screamed before, but that day I was unstoppable. 'Help, help,' I yelled.

I had no idea what was on the end of my line, but the sheer weight was pulling me overboard. People were trying to cut the line but they couldn't get through because of the waves. I thought I was going to lose my fingers or even get dragged under. Eventually, after what appeared to be a lifetime, my friend Savid managed to cut the line. I experienced a pain I've never had in my life before. The line had cut right through my skin and I could see the bone on three of the fingers. I was in agony. There was blood everywhere. At first Kate couldn't believe what was happening.

No one wanted to play the hero, but it was agreed we should try to find out what was on the end of my line. After hunting around they eventually found a massive manta ray. At first they wanted to kill it, but I thought that was wrong. After all, they're beautiful creatures.

I was taken straight to hospital, where I had stitches on my hand. But I learned a good lesson that day! I don't care how people do it locally, next time I go fishing I want proper rope gloves. Oh, and I'll never cross the lines. But it was certainly something to remember.

Harvey and Junior stayed with us throughout the whole honeymoon. I wish we'd taken a nanny because caring for two kids became exhausting. Junior was still waking up a lot through the night and Harvey constantly needed his medication. We couldn't just go out or take a nap whenever we wanted. But it was beautiful to have the family together and I think we needed that.

There was one Japanese restaurant on the island that seemed to be in the middle of nowhere. You had to walk through bushes to find it. They were playing the most amazing and romantic Japanese music. I asked the staff to make me a tape. Back at the villa, Kate and I would lie on the balcony and make love, our CD playing in the background. The stars shone so brightly in the clear sky. It was the first time Kate had seen the Milky Way. It really was a beautiful honeymoon.

CHAPTER NINETEEN

TRUST

ALTHOUGH BEING MARRIED and having children has always been one of my greatest ambitions, it's a lifestyle I could not have imagined ten years ago. I simply wasn't ready. But over time my priorities have changed. I now respect women a lot more and, most importantly, I respect myself. None of this could have happened had it not been for my breakdown. But every day I thank God that I was lucky to meet Kate at the right moment in my life.

There are many things I regret about my past, but none of us can turn back the clock. While I'm eager to move on with my future, Kate is determined never to let me forget my past. Her obsession with my ex-girlfriends is beyond ridiculous. Even girls I've held hands with have felt the force of Kate's fury. Her jealousy and insecurity have been the cause of so many problems in our relationship. No matter how hard I try to convince her, she simply can't believe that I have eyes only for her.

I did sleep with a lot of girls. I was terrible. I was an arsehole. I didn't intend to hurt anybody, but it was all about my satisfaction. It was something Kate and I spoke about from the start. She asked me how many women I'd slept with and I said, 'Kate, honestly? I don't know.'

'What do you mean, you don't know,' she replied, shocked and hurt.

Guys are arseholes, because we go through a stage where it's anyone and everyone. We don't think about consequences, about pregnancies and diseases. It's unfair because a woman does it and she's labelled a slut, whereas a man does it and he's a legend. The main reason guys sleep around is to impress their mates. Nobody needs sex that much unless they have a serious problem. When you find someone you genuinely love and you're at the stage when you want to have kids and settle down, you suddenly think, Oh my God, what have I been doing all my life?

I have no right to be upset about Kate's past. The thought of anyone being as intimate with her as I am makes me feel really angry. But I accept it. I have nothing against her ex, Scott. She wasn't happy with him. Goodbye. See you later. That's the way it works in this world. Dane Bowers – now I believe they had a lot of arguments but Dane was in a group called Another Level and they opened for me at Wembley, so we were all mates.

The night before Kate left for the jungle she did something which no one knows about. It's a secret that I'm going to share. It partly explains why I find it so hard to trust her unconditionally. Before Kate met me she used to go out and get drunk all the time. She promises me she's never had a one-night stand. Even if she was completely off her face, she swears, she would never sleep with someone. There's a guy she went to a club with the night before she flew to Australia and this guy was from a well-known boy band. That night they both sloped off to the toilets and got up to some naughty things. She told me she never slept with him, but as far as I'm concerned she may as well have done. What's the difference? Besides, wasn't she meant to be seeing Scott? Kate told me that she had never cheated on anyone but, to me, this was just as bad.

I'd met this pop star briefly before and I have to say he's a really nice guy and a good bloke. I'm not happy that we've shared the same woman. The fact is, if Kate had to come face to face with any woman I'd even held hands with, she would be utterly hostile towards her. Whereas I've seen this particular guy since then. Yet I don't like him any less. He didn't know that I was going to meet Kate, fall in love with her and marry her. He's happy in a relationship now, but Kate won't talk to him because she feels it's disrespectful to me. But to me it's not fair that I can be grown up enough to deal with my insecurities but she can't.

Every girl I'm with, she'll ask, 'Have you done anything with her? Have you kissed her? Swear on your life?' She has this strange sense about girls. But she gets the information out of me and then holds it against me. Kate upset a lot of people with her book. She made a reference to twins I'd once slept with. It was horrible.

We both get jealous, but I do think Kate takes it too far. I can't even comment on a good video clip because she'll think I'm looking at the dancers. She suffers from a massive insecurity. Some guy must have really f****d her up in the past! These days I'm a lot more relaxed. I used to do everything for myself – training, image, it was all me, me, me. The fact that I've left all that behind shows her I'm content; that I've got no intention of going anywhere.

I am a jealous person myself, but I do think she takes it a notch too far. If she doesn't give me reason to distrust her, I trust her, because I trust myself so much now. When you trust yourself, you're a lot more likely to trust someone else.

Despite Kate's insecurities about my ex-girlfriends, her ex Dwight Yorke will always play a big role in our lives. Of course, I love Harvey more than anything in the world and I hate to use him as an example, but his real dad will be involved in our lives for ever. That's about the biggest reminder of a past relationship you can get. The difference is, I can handle that.

Here's where I have an issue. Recently, I'd let myself go a little bit. I'm currently training, so I'm not worried, but I do still have my insecurities. Kate has made it very clear to girls that they should keep away from me. They never approach me any more and I don't know whether it's because I've completely lost it or because they're scared of Kate. We might go out and I'll be dressed up and feeling confident and a few girls will come up to us, but they'll all be talking to Kate. Surely I haven't become that unattractive? There are occasions when Kate will go to the bathroom and that's when someone will talk to me. It's not because I'm interested in other girls, but it is a nice feeling.

Kate's glamour modelling has never bothered me one little bit. She's the best at her job. She knows how to put on the persona. I've never once told her what to wear or what work to do. My only request is that she control her drinking habits. We are both jealous and insecure characters by nature and we struggle to keep control of our fears. The best way round it is to be honest with each other. We always leave our phones lying around and I'm more than happy for Kate to read through my messages. I have nothing to hide. To be honest, I trust her to never look. Yet there was one time, I'm ashamed to say, when my paranoia got the better of me.

One night she was really drunk at the house with her friend Sally. She rang me at 3am and slurred, 'Pete, we're gonna get a cab to Neil's house.'

Neil is one of her mates from the past who happens to have a great body. Kate and Sally were already planning to have some treatments the next day at a salon close to his house. 'Like f**k you're gonna stay at Neil's house,' I said through gritted teeth.

'All right, all right, I won't go,' she said. But she was off her face and in that state she never thinks. I convinced myself that she was lying to me and that she would already be on her way over there in a cab. So an hour later I called our home and there was no answer. I was really pissed off. It's the only time in our relationship I didn't trust her. Only one time!

The next day when I got home, she promised me that all she'd done was go outside to our garage to fetch some drinks. During the ten minutes I was trying to get through, she was outside and unable to hear her phone. I didn't believe her at first.

'OK, go and check the cameras!' she challenged me.

'You know what,' I said. 'You've told me a million times to go and check the cameras and this time I'm gonna do it. If I keep saying no, you'll use it against me.'

So I did. I went and checked the cameras and I wanted to give her the biggest hug afterwards. Running back through the footage, I saw her go outside and into the garage and ten minutes later come back out with a lot of different drinks. I carried on watching and she didn't leave for the rest of the night. No one came and left. I felt really bad, but I was glad I did it because now she knows that there could be a time when I will check.

'Now apologise,' she demanded.

I'm not sure if Kate has ever checked the cameras on me. I'm not sure she'd know how to! She knows my routines so well. I get up in the morning and have a coffee, then go in the studio to do a bit of music. And when I'm working she knows exactly where I am because we have the same manager. I don't go and hang out with my friends and my family live overseas. And still I get battered when we go out if I even so much as glance at a girl.

One thing about Kate is that she's a very loving woman and I don't think she'd ever intentionally hurt me. I say that because she was the woman I thought I'd never trust. I've trusted other women whom I should never have trusted. Kate, who one would expect to be the wildest of them all, who has everything at her feet and can have anyone and anything she wants, is the one I trust the most. I think a lot of that is because I trust myself at last. This is why she's very scared of me leaving her – not because I'm anybody special, but because she's obviously been through some bad times and I don't know how much of herself she believes in.

It's all about trusting your own character. The minute you start feeling comfortable with yourself, you start seeing things differently – and I can't wait for the day it happens to Kate. She might have to step away from this industry for a while, like I did. I kind of hope she doesn't because she's on top of the world at the moment and her work is going great. But sometimes you have to step away. I'm living proof of that.

I do see this girl differently from the way I see everyone else and I do wake up with the most sought-after woman in Britain and, in my eyes, the most beautiful. But I won't put up with certain attitudes just because of who she is, and she knows that. At the same time I like to think I'm a very loving and caring husband. I'm always asking her if she has eaten. I want to make sure she's looked after in every way. I don't want her to ever go without anything – whether she can afford it or not. She would starve some days if I wasn't here to make her dinner. She could go all day without eating, because she forgets to. It's only a little thing, but I will make sure that at least once a day I cook something so that I know that she has eaten. She looks after me too in different ways – by being a great mum and giving me a lot of love. Of course, we have our issues like all married couples but, most importantly, I love Kate to bits.

CHAPTER TWENTY

THE DEMON DRINK

I TRUST KATE more than anyone in the world. There's only one thing that causes me to question her honesty – and that's drink.

When I used to see girls drunk in clubs, it always meant one thing to me: you or one of your mates is going to get laid tonight. It's a bad attitude to have, but I was a lot younger and arrogant in those days. Drink removed your inhibitions and made you more likely to do things. I always associated drink and clubs with sex. That's a chapter of my life I closed years ago and it's not one I intend to reopen.

There are several reasons why I don't drink any more. The main one is that several years ago it almost killed me. Soon after my breakdown, when I returned to our resort in Australia, we held a party there for New Year's Eve and I got smashed. One of the girls we worked with was coming on to me, so I took her into one of the rooms. At that point I told my friends and family I was going to bed. As I stumbled back into the party I felt a familiar wave of nausea pass over me. For the first time in months I was experiencing a panic attack – only this time I had even less control over what was going on because I was drunk.

I thought I was going to die. I started shaking and I couldn't breathe. It was one of the worst attacks I'd ever had. I crawled into one of the rooms and somehow I made it through the night alone. The very next day I decided I'd never drink again. That was 2002 and I don't think I've ever been drunk since. At first I couldn't understand people getting drunk. Then I started to envy them. I almost feel like I'm still being taught a lesson – that it might happen to me again, only this time I won't be so lucky. Every time I go to have a drink, something taps me on the shoulder and reminds me what happened that night. There are so many nights when I really want to get drunk with my friends and have a good night, but I can't do it. I'm really sad about that. That's one part of my life where I think I've grown up too soon.

My second fear about drinking is linked to infidelity. I remember one particular girlfriend I was with in Japan when I was 17. I was working in a cabaret club as a Michael Jackson impersonator when I first met Kimberly, who was a lot older than me. The record company had suggested I take the job out there while they waited for the right time to release my first single in Australia. We were staying in a really dodgy part called Hanazono Cho, in Osaka, where the Japanese mafia are rife. At 3am every morning you'd hear them tearing up and down the road on their motorbikes just to let you know they're there.

Kimberly was an escort girl and she arrived with a rich businessman. I knew she was instantly mesmerised by my show and she kept requesting a repeat performance. Afterwards I introduced myself and before long we were seeing each other.

I started to really like her, even though she thought I was just a little kid. Eventually she became very possessive and I became her little toyboy who stayed in the house. She had me under lock and key. She became so obsessive that she would follow me wherever I went. Then she started checking through my phone bills. One time she rang a number in Australia and a girl answered. I came home and the whole house was in darkness. Suddenly she lunged at me from the shadows, screaming, 'You fucking bastard.' She went for me, but I turned and ran. I picked up a table and threw it at her before leaving the house.

The problem was, she loved to drink and whenever she was drunk her personality would suddenly switch. Another night we'd been drinking in a club and we had an argument.

'Fuck you, I'm going home,' she hissed at me.

I knew she was desperate for revenge. I stayed at the club, but when I finally arrived home she couldn't wait for me to see her in bed with this other man. Deep in my heart I didn't love her, but from then on my attitude towards drink was a problem.

I've had ex-girlfriends who would drink and I didn't mind because they actually became more clingy towards me. I used to love it. But when Kate drinks she becomes distant, aggressive, arrogant and flirtatious. She reminds me a lot of Kimberly. The devil gets inside her. She's told me about what she was like before she met me and how she would tease guys to the point of almost sleeping with them before laughing in their face and walking away.

Kate also had a reputation for insulting celebrities in the press. I remember the run-up to the Eurovision Song Contest when she'd start abusing a girl called Javine. Then there were people like Jodie Marsh.

These people had slated her in the press, but Kate would wait until we were out somewhere, get drunk and call them sluts to their faces, and the whole night would be spoiled. It's horrible and I find it very hard to deal with.

She's so non-flirty when she's sober. Her life is her husband, her kids and her work, but when she gets drunk she has the confidence to be who she obviously wants to be and that person is a flirt, abusive and arrogant. Why would I want her to be like that? That's Jordan, not the Kate I know and love.

Often Kate forgets I'm even there. She becomes a completely different person and I have to keep my eye on her at all times. For example, I clearly remember an incident with Rebecca Loos. We were at a Chinese New Year party hosted by Andy Wong and Kate had gone out with every determination to get smashed, to outdo everyone else in her see-through dress. All night Rebecca kept coming up to me and saying, 'I'll do anything to feel Kate's body, to touch her breasts and to feel her arse.'

'Rebecca!' I said, thinking she was a bit over the top.

'Hottest body in the world!' she went on.

But, because Kate was so smashed, she didn't have a clue what was going on. Rebecca kept asking her if she wanted to go to the toilet – because girls always go together. I had this horrible fear that she was taking advantage of Kate.

Now I should trust Kate, but that night upset me. They were in there for nearly half an hour. I don't care how long a girl takes to put powder on her face – but it can't take that long! That night we had the biggest row. I said to her, 'You'd better hope to God that Rebecca doesn't do a story on you saying she has done intimate things with you in the bathroom. There's not a question about it. Even if it didn't happen. You would never go to the bathroom with her if you were sober. You'd be like, "I don't want to talk to her!" God knows what she's intending to do to you.' I now know that what I said was a result of my insecurities but, if Kate had not got drunk in the first place, none of this would ever have happened.

One time we were in Dubai. During the day Kate refused to see anybody. 'I fucking hate everyone,' she complained. We'd go into a mall and she'd hide behind pillars to avoid any fans who might ask for an autograph. But that night she'd be off her face in a bar full of Brits, singing to them with her arms around them.

These were the same people she couldn't stand in the day. That's a complete change. I've said to her, 'Kate, I love you with all my heart but I'm not a pushover. You might have had your way with all these other guys, but you're not going out with a kid any more.'

She was swearing at the staff in Dubai who are all Muslim, saying things like, 'Your husband's a tosser to treat you like that.'

One of the bar staff said to me, 'Aren't you going to hold her so she doesn't fall over?'

'I hope she falls flat on her face and makes a fool of herself,' I replied.

Sometimes when there are photographers around I wish she would fall over, just so she can see what's she's like the next day. Yet she radiates such beauty when she's herself. We've got kids now. I'm not asking her not to have a drink. I'd just rather she didn't have ten! Luckily, nowadays, this is very rare, thank goodness.

I know that deep inside she doesn't want to become that person but she does it because she lacks confidence sometimes. That's why she never drinks at home, because there she's relaxed and confident. One thing that upsets me so much is that I'd hoped that she could have me next to her and that would give her confidence. Not a bottle.

I'm not jealous of anybody until Kate is drunk. There is nobody that I feel threatened by when she's sober. But if she's drunk I know she's capable of doing anything. One night we had sex in the stables and we went absolutely nuts. She was off her face. It was the only time she's been drunk at home.

'I'm gonna f**k you in the stables,' she said.

'Right, tonight it's raw, dirty and there's no respect,' I told her.

We went into the stables and we were wild. We did everything. The next day I said to her, 'That was nice in the stables.'

'What?' she said, as if she had no idea what I was talking about. 'What do you mean? We didn't have sex.'

'We had more than sex,' I told her. 'We did everything.'

'You're winding me up!' she laughed. She genuinely

246

didn't have a clue what I was talking about. Imagine how it makes me feel to know that she's capable of anything when she's completely drunk.

She has improved, but when she does get smashed it's always one drink too many. It has got to the point where I don't want to see it any more, so I've suggested she go out alone with her girlfriends. The only reason she won't – and this is the truth – is because she doesn't want me to go out with my friends. I've told her I'm willing to not go out with my friends – I don't have that many anyway – and she can still go out with her girlfriends. But still she won't.

Our relationship shouldn't just be about me compromising over everything. She needs to compromise too. I have put up with no sex for months, an ex who can come into our lives at any time, the knowledge that she didn't want to hold Junior for the first six months because of her post-natal depression – all of it, but I get through it because of the strength of my love for Kate.

All I ask is one thing. Please don't get smashed. This isn't about anyone else – it's about us.

CHAPTER TWENTY-ONE

UNDER SIEGE

I'VE ALWAYS CONSIDERED family to be my number-one priority, but since becoming a husband and father I now value the people close to me even more. If anything ever happened to Kate or the kids, I'd be devastated. My life would fall apart. Fortunately, in the past I've never been given cause to worry. As far as I was concerned, nothing could touch us. But in April 2006 a threat was made to my family and I realised just how vulnerable we really are.

It was 8pm and Kate and I were just about to go out for a bite to eat, when the doorbell rang at the front gate. We weren't expecting anyone.

'Who's that?' I said.

Kate picked up the camera phone.

'Hello, I'm Detective Steve Johns from Sussex Police,' said a gentleman in a smart suit and a trench coat. 'I need to talk to you.'

'But how do I know you're really a policeman?' asked Kate suspiciously.

He flashed his badge at the camera. Kate and I are both cautious and she still wasn't convinced. After all, anyone could make a fake badge. But, despite her misgivings, Kate decided to let him in through the first gate.

'Pete, there's an officer here who wants to speak to us.'

By now he had reached the front door.

'Do you have any plans for this evening?' he asked.

'We were just about to go out for dinner, but don't worry about it,' I said.

Looking stern, he replied, 'You won't want to go when you hear what I have to tell you.'

By now I was really confused. Someone is obviously planning to break into the house tonight, I thought.

'Do you want to call another police officer to make sure I'm genuine?' he asked.

'That's a good idea,' I agreed.

I rang the local station and spoke to an officer called Kathy. She ran a check and verified the detective's details.

'Yes, this man is a police officer,' she reassured us. 'My sergeant knows him very well.'

Still Kate and I weren't completely convinced. What if this man was an impostor who had stolen the detective's badge? When you live in a world like ours, you have to be so careful. Thoughts like that run constantly through your mind. However, at least now the police were aware this man had entered our house.

We all sat down in the living room. I could feel a real tension mounting in the room.

'I can't tell you exactly what's going on,' he continued. 'But all I can say is that four officers from Scotland Yard are on their way to your house and you've got to stay here.'

That statement sent shivers down my spine. I've got to be honest, I was frightened. It's not the kind of thing you hear every day. It was like a scene from a movie.

All of a sudden more officers were at the gates, all of them dressed in plain clothes suits. Either these guys are genuine or we're completely screwed, I thought.

'I'm going to ring Claire,' I said to Kate. 'We need someone else at the house.'

No matter how personal it might be, I thought our management should be involved. If something drastic had happened they would need to change our schedules and, besides, it's always good to have a witness.

All along Kate thought it was a wind-up.

'C'mon then, where's Jeremy Beadle?' she joked. 'Where are the cameras?'

It was annoying me because I knew these guys were serious. I could tell they were genuine.

Another, more menacing, man introduced himself. 'I'm Detective Alan Pughsley. Please sit down,' he said.

Kate and I looked at each other in silence.

'I'm just going to be blunt with you,' he continued. 'I don't know how you're going to take what I have to tell you.'

'Are you all right with this kind of news?' another officer asked Kate. 'Are you OK with us saying it straight out or do you want us to warm you into it?'

By now I was feeling uncomfortable.

'Speaking of warm,' I interrupted, 'how about I make you all a cup of coffee?'

I knew they had something serious to tell us and I wanted to break the ice. Besides, I'm a coffee freak. It's a comfort thing.

'Just tell Kate what subject we're talking about and I'll be back in a sec.'

We wanted to wait for Claire and Neville to arrive. Then they told us straight.

'We can't divulge any names, but we've received a tip-off from an informant. There's been a conversation and a plot has been discussed to kidnap one or both of your children.'

Straight away I clenched up inside at the thought of anyone even coming near my kids. I felt a horrible acidic taste of nausea rise from my stomach and up into my mouth. What had seemed like a surreal movie script was now turning into a horrible reality. My mind was whirling. Suddenly I started thinking, What, where, how, who?

Up until that point Kate had remained adamant that we were all playing a trick on her and any minute now a film crew would leap out to record her reaction.

'Will you please take this seriously?' I hissed. Claire swore that this was no wind-up.

But when she heard the word 'children' she froze. She knew we wouldn't mess around with a topic like that. She started fidgeting nervously in her chair and tapping her face with her hands.

We all began bombarding the police with questions.

They believed four people were involved. That was all the information they had. They had to tell us now for the kids' safety. From what they could tell, the kidnap would take place when Kate was out with the boys. They would wait until she was driving, run her off the road and then take one or both of them. They wouldn't do anything while I was in the car, because it would be much harder to execute the plan with a male there. They had discussed everything in minute detail; for instance, exactly how they would force Kate off the road and how far away from the house they would do it. These people knew so much – they even knew what cars we were driving, where we go shopping, Harvey's school, Junior's day centre... It was scary.

Scotland Yard had no idea when the kidnappers were planning to act, but the conversation had taken place recently. From now on we would have to keep the boys indoors and, if we were to step outside, a police offer would have to accompany us.

We weren't allowed to tell anyone what was going on, but I needed to speak to someone, so I got straight on the phone to my brother Michael. He was even planning to quit his job and come and stay with me. By now I was feeling very emotional and overwhelmed. I was in a state of shock and not quite sure how to react.

A kidnap plot involving your family is a devastating thought, but so surreal it only hits you as days go by. It hits you when you're just about to get in the car and pop into town for a bit of shopping with the kids. All of a sudden you have to think twice.

Straight away I told Claire to cancel everything in my schedule for the next few days. I was going to stay at home with the children and I didn't care. Over my dead body, I thought. No one will ever come within a hair's distance of my sons. As long as Harvey and Junior were at home, the officer assured us, they would be safe.

Kate had a trip to China planned. At first she wanted to cancel it, but I encouraged her to go. I thought that, if she was away, the likelihood of anything happening would be less as she was the person they were targeting. I was supposed to go with her to Shanghai, but in the present situation I decided to stay at home.

'You've got to go,' I told Kate firmly. I think it was the best thing she could have done.

Twenty-four-hour security was put in place. It still is and will be for a long time. Normally I wouldn't discuss a sensitive matter like this in public, but those who thought of attacking our family will have to think again. We are under constant surveillance by Scotland Yard and are 100 per cent reassured of our safety. Our lives had to really change, but we managed to keep the whole thing under wraps for eight weeks. We got stick for cancelling some things but our kids and our safety come first and we didn't want the press to know. Unfortunately, the *News of the World* found out but we never commented on the situation.

Kate had been through a tough time in the past few months and was in a very fragile state. The last thing she needed was this. Her little relaxation is taking the kids into Brighton and wandering round the shops. She never goes alone now. Whether a security guard is standing right next to her or ten metres behind, she's never out of their sight.

It was a horrible time. My mind was in overdrive. What if the informant got something wrong? What if the plan had already been set in motion? People were inviting me out and I'd have to make excuses. Kate was in Shanghai and I felt really alone. I was devastated. I wasn't allowed to tell anyone and yet every day I could picture a disaster happening. I started living a nightmare.

I didn't want to take the kids out, but at the same time I didn't want them stuck in the house. Kate and I were constantly on the phone to each other but I felt that the longer she stayed in Shanghai the better. At least it would give the police more time to investigate and without her in the country the plan couldn't be set in motion. To add to our pressures, the press were constantly questioning why my wife was in China without me. After all, they knew we didn't like to be apart for any period of time. They were puzzled and reports began to emerge that we were having problems and our marriage was in danger. If only they'd known the truth. I missed Kate but at least I had my kids in my hands. Nothing would happen to them while they were in my care. It was the longest that Kate and I had ever been apart and we hated it; we phoned each other about 20 times a day.

A situation like this makes you realise you're not untouchable. I never really understood what David and Victoria Beckham went through when a kidnap threat was made on Brooklyn, but now I fully understand. The police asked us if we'd like to make a statement to the press but we declined. We agreed it would be better if any official statements came from Scotland Yard. That way, any potential attackers would take us more seriously.

I've always been protective towards the children but this whole episode has definitely made me a lot more cautious.

There's this thing called counter-surveillance where you survey people who are surveying you. When you're driving you check your rear-view mirrors to see if anyone is following you. When you go round a roundabout and you think someone is following you, you go round twice or take a different exit from the one you would normally use. These are things I'd never had to do before. Unfortunately, you need to have your wits about you or you're finished. So, once again, I was looking over my shoulder.

It was a difficult time, but we knew we had to fight through it. I was getting constant aches in my back. It was something I've never experienced before and the doctor put it down to stress. Initially the whole situation put a real strain on us. We started putting a lot of security in place – why didn't we have it before? Even so, after a time, a threat like this does bring you closer.

The danger to our children is still there, but I know the risk factor is low. We are in constant contact with the police. I try to imagine how these sick people's minds might work. Whenever someone approaches me for an autograph I automatically think, Should I be talking to them? It's horrible because I'm such a sociable person.

Kate and I both love England and we never want to leave the country. The people here have been so good to us. To be honest, even in Cyprus I worry for the boys' safety. I'm having top-of-the-range security systems installed in our house.

As I've said before, I always try to look for the positive side to any situation. During that dark period when Kate travelled to China and I stayed at home, there was one great thing that happened. I've helped with Harvey's medicine in the past, but I've never done the injection myself. But during that week I did it for the first time ever. Now Kate and I take it in turns, although I still don't like the fact that he has to be injected. It was my way of learning and it brought me closer to Harvey. In fact, in trying to break our family apart, those people brought all four of us closer together.

CHAPTER TWENTY TWO

IN HARMONY

THANKFULLY, I NO longer have the constant drive and determination that once made me hungry for pop success. I'm still very driven, but not obsessed. I've since found a new role in life as father and husband and I've never felt so content. But I've never given up on music. Over the past few years I've written hundreds of songs and it's my dream that one day I'll be able to release them on my own terms. People have never heard what I'm really capable of and for once I'd like to be judged for myself.

A lot of people have heard me sing songs like 'Mysterious Girl' and 'Insania', but those are songs I wouldn't even play in my car now. I listen to old soul, jazz and blues – people like Anita Baker, George Benson, Quincy Jones. I grew up on that. But those are never the songs record companies want me to release. People relate to me as the 'six pack who sings' and that's the way it is. Maybe if I was as hungry as I was in the past I'd be so much more determined, but now I'm just writing and enjoying it.

After the jungle I had three weeks to release an album. It was a bit of a joke! Besides, the record company weren't particularly interested in anything I'd written. They wanted to recoup some of the money they'd lost on my *Time* album. To be honest, I don't blame them.

We had a bit of a nightmare while trying to shoot the video for 'Insania'. We went to Madrid so that we could film in the sunshine – and ended up shooting most of it indoors because the weather was so poor! In fact, it rained so much that we couldn't put the roof down on the open-top car we were using for the shoot. When it got to 2am and we were all cold and wet, they had to put covers over the car and heaters inside it to stop us from freezing. Kerrie Ann, my stylist, and Claire were great and trooped everywhere to find us coffee and soup to keep us going. How we suffered for our art!

After Kate and I recorded 'A Whole New World' for Children In Need, we knew instantly that it would be a hit. Initially, the charity asked us to do ballroom dancing, but Kate and I thought that was too tacky; and, as neither of us can do ballroom dancing, we knew it would look dreadful. Then she came up with the idea of doing the song. It was something we both believed in and it was for a good cause. For once, I thought, people would hear me sing a powerful ballad. Our performance brought a huge response and the phone lines were jammed. People loved it. The very next day all the major labels were calling Claire and asking for it to be released it as a single.

Claire and Neville went to see several record companies and agreed that they could only have a 'Duets' album if they also offered Kate and me solo deals. As fate would have it,

I've had an opportunity to record a duet on every album, but I've never done it. Now I have the opportunity to record one for the first time – with my wife.

We've been working on the album with Nicky Graham and Denni Lew. Nicky Graham used to be very high up at Sony and was responsible for the Bros album and parts of my first album. We love them as people and they're great producers.

Kate is so excited. Singing has always been a major ambition of hers and I know how desperate she is to have a successful pop career. If I'm completely honest, I never wanted Kate to do Eurovision. I didn't think it would be a good launchpad for a musical career. However, I don't think she wanted to do it either. There was a deal on the table and she was pushed in a corner. The song was great, but it wasn't suited to Kate. She didn't feel comfortable with it at all. But I wanted to support her the whole way.

On the night of the competition I felt a bit left out because I wanted to give her certain advice, but everyone else in the room was having their say. Instead, I stood outside. I couldn't get to her then anyway, because there was too much going on. When I heard her sing I didn't think it was a great performance as she had a panic attack before she went on stage. I couldn't stand the outfit either! She was pregnant and it didn't look right at all. But I wasn't about to discourage her before she went on stage. She did Eurovision because she had to, not because she wanted to, and that's why she regrets it so much. I think, if Claire had known she was pregnant earlier, she would have pulled her out of the competition for sure.

Kate knew she had to buckle down and get her vocals

happening. She could sing, but only when she was ready. I need her to have the confidence to sing any time and any place. I'm trying to encourage Kate to come into the studio when I'm writing, but she tends to come in when it's time to practise her vocals. We've both been having singing lessons, me for years and Katie for the past year. I think Kate has the passion; it's just the technique she needs to work on. She has come on so much and so quickly in the past few months. Kate can sing when she's concentrating. In the beginning she could be very lazy and on occasion was texting at the same time as she was singing. But she's getting better and better. Initially I was worried that she might be doing this simply to put another notch on her belt. But over time she started calling for more singing lessons. Kate is a very determined person and she doesn't give up easily. I know she really wants a singing career and I believe she really deserves it. The effort started to show at the end of last year before we did Children In Need.

I am protective of Kate because I don't think she realises how cut-throat this industry is. People are waiting for you to make the slightest mistake. It's full of empty promises and you'll always think you're not good enough. Kate is stronger than a lot of people and she can take knockbacks, so I think she'll be able to cope with it. My priorities are different now, but I know how much Kate wants this to work, and I want to support her all the way.

CHAPTER TWENTY-THREE

ALL ABOUT US

DESPITE OUR ARGUMENTS, married life with Kate has been everything I ever imagined – and more. Whenever I leave the house for a job I can't wait to rush back home to my wife and children. Kate and I still try to spend as much time together as we can and we hate to be apart. Recently, we were sitting together on the couch watching TV; she sits on one side because the radiator is right behind her, while I sit on the other side because I find the house too hot. But we hate being apart, so we stretched our legs just enough so our toes touched. That's just the way we are. We're very much in love and I know we'd be lost without each other.

One of mine and Kate's favourite (non-sexual) games is re-enacting *X-Factor* auditions. Kate makes me come into the front room as several different characters – a north London builder or a sleazy Italian or a chauvinistic Greek or a Mexican who can hardly speak English. She changes roles as either Sharon or Kate as she would be on the show. Then

263

I make her get up and I pretend to be either Simon Cowell or Louis or how I would be.

We have each other in absolute fits. Sometimes I walk in with my trousers right up under my chest and my hair parted on the side. Other times I'll wear glasses or be a hard-core rapper. We have such a laugh. Kate tries to be the Celine Dion type or a Barbie doll and act the real dumb blonde. She loves to act out scenes but she has such a blatant Brighton accent I can always tell it's her. Once we did a TV show where they made Kate look like an old woman. I could so tell it was her from her voice. We have such a good laugh. It's so amazing that we can be such great mates, such amazing lovers *and* married with kids.

Another love we share is food. That's a topic we discuss a lot. Recently I've developed a keen interest in cooking. Every night I experiment with a different recipe. Whenever we go out to eat, the food has to be perfect. We love all flavours and will try any type of food. Apart from when she was using her fitness video after Junior was born, I've never seen Kate diet. She doesn't worry about the food she eats. She'll put away a fair amount and I love that. I've been in relationships where the girl picks at a salad, but I couldn't complain because I used to do the same. But how good is it later in life when you and your partner let yourselves go and you enjoy your time together.

As a married couple we do a lot of staying at home with a cup of tea in front of the TV. We go as normal as pie at night! Honestly. Another of our favourite pastimes is playing board games. Katie loves Monopoly. She always buys property when she knows she can't! She wants to win everything and sometimes she's a bit of a cheat. I suppose she's too much of a fighter to give up. She's done the occasional, 'Oh, I'm going to bed, I'm really tired' when she's losing!

Another favourite is Trivial Pursuit. I can't play the Genius Edition – forget it! The Kids' Edition is a little too easy, but the Family Edition is pretty good. I love the blatant wrong answers. Kate can be so sharp, but ask her a general knowledge question and she wouldn't have a clue. I think that's cute. I'll ask her something like, 'What's an eclipse?' and she'll reply, 'Oh, how stupid, it's an ice cream!' I'll think she's joking, but she's not and that's what's so endearing!

She really makes me laugh sometimes. For instance, she'll try to say the word 'psychologist' but she'll never be able to pronounce it properly. Instead, she'll say something like 'phisiotologist'. Or she'll use a big word that has absolutely no relevance to a sentence. I'll say something like, 'Babes, how are you feeling today?' and she'll reply, 'Well, like any woman feels. It's our prerogative!'

'What?'

'It's our prerogative.'

'Can you define what the word "prerogative" means, please?'

'Oh, shut up, Pete. You know I don't know what it means!'

I tell you, those are the moments I just want to grab her. I love her so much. She's so honest, genuine and naive. In that respect, she reminds me of my sister; girls like that don't let guys get away with anything, they're so focused on what's right and wrong, but ask them what 12 times 12 is and they'll spend hours trying to figure it out. Kate fascinates me. Baby, I love you, but how can you be so smart in so many ways and so thick in so many others! Another time she wanted to say 'colonic irrigation' and she said 'chronic irritation'. God bless you, babes!

I'm also about to start horse-riding lessons. I'm determined to go riding with Kate in Ashdown Forest. The countryside around where we live is beautiful. We love going for walks and holding hands, but the truth of the matter is, Kate hates walking anywhere. If she had it her way, the dogs would walk and she'd drive in the car next to them. I've been trying to persuade her to come to the gym with me. OK, she already has an amazing body, but mentally she'd really benefit from a regular work-out.

One of the only things Kate and I don't have in common is our tastes in movies. I absolutely love comedies but she doesn't. She loves psychological thrillers, and that's all she'll watch at home. She'll watch *The FBI Files*, *The Cold Case Files*, *The Murder Files* – everything to do with murders. She reads books about how killers like Fred and Rosemary West, Dennis Nilsen or Charles Manson carved their victims up.

'You know what, I could commit the perfect murder!' she once said to me.

'Well, no, you can't, because you've just told me,' I laughed.

She makes me laugh with her innocence and naivety. She's very smart, witty and cool. She can be elegant and girlie and then she can be so common and stick up her finger at someone who's just cut her up on the road or eff and blind with the best. She has two sides to her. When she's in her own home environment she's the most relaxed person. When she's doing her job she's the queen and no one can touch her. Somehow she manages to separate the two when she gets home. She'll run in, put on her old trackie pants and slump down on the couch. It pisses me off that she always looks good! Even in the crappiest outfit, with her hair a mess and no make-up, she still looks a million dollars.

Yes, Gary, you do a great job, but I still prefer Kate without any make-up. She's such a natural stunner. Kate is one of these people who will never believe she is as good as she actually is and that's what I love about her. Rather than having an inflated ego, she's extremely humble. The only problem is, some people mistake her insecurity for bad manners. Often she shies away from people because she doesn't want them to see her up close. She becomes really snobby, although that's never her intention. The reason people think she loves herself is because deep down she hates herself! It's so ironic. She's a great mother, easily the most dynamic woman I've been with sexually and she stimulates my mind.

I love to talk about science and technology. I'm fascinated by phenomena like UFOs or what happens after death. Kate loves to hear me talk about history and the Bible. I might not know about civil wars and dates, but I'm very interested in events from the past and the future possibilities. Kate will sit on the sofa and constantly fire questions at me.

'Babe, I'm not that bloody smart!' I tell her.

When Kate is out and about, I hear her talk so much about her hair and her nails. That's fair enough – after all, it is an important part of her work as a model! But at home she talks about the simple things, like sewing. She loves sewing and makes a lot of Harvey's and Junior's clothes. It's a hobby she's had for a long time. She has a machine and patterns and she's always popping down to Brighton to collect new materials.

Kate is a lot more domesticated than when I first met her, that's for sure! I'm obsessed about keeping the house clean, but I would never expect someone else to do what I was unwilling to do myself. Kate is the kind of girl who will put her rubber gloves on and wander round the kitchen. The difference is, she will purposefully do the housework in the tiniest little mini skirt she can find – just to tease me! She constantly tries to wind me up by doing the vacuuming in a tiny pair of hot pants.

I've shared so many wonderful and new experiences with Kate. I celebrated my first Christmas here two years ago. We both went nuts and bought each other so many gifts. We had a couple of big ones and then some little things which had more thought to them. If Kate likes a certain artist, say, I'll make her a tape of all their music, along with an information pack about them. Last Christmas I gave her helicopter lessons because she wanted to learn how to fly. She bought me vouchers for rally driving and hot-air ballooning. Our big presents are always jewellery.

I remember our first Christmas Day vividly. Lunch was great – we had a bird in a bird in a bird. Kate is one hell of a cook, and I've never had a better roast than hers, except my sister-in-law Pam's – she makes an awesome 'Pam roast'. Kate likes to set the presents around the tree. It was all quite overwhelming for me, because I couldn't understand how one person could receive so many gifts. I almost felt shy about opening them. However, Kate gave me one of my funniest presents in front of the cameras as part of our documentary.

She'd hired real reindeer and a sleigh and was planning to dress up as Mrs Santa Claus and surprise me.

'I've got a surprise for you. Wait till you see it!' she told me.

'This surprise, can I use it?' I asked her.

'Yes, but not straight away.'

'Is it something I can keep?'

'If you're good to it, of course you can!'

'Is it something I can ride?'

'Yes.'

Is it a quad bike? What is it? Then she turned up in a sleigh with all these reindeer and screamed, 'Surprise!' I honestly thought she'd bought me a reindeer. 'Wow,' I said. All I could think was, I can't ride that! Meanwhile, she was going, 'Hello, hello', and I said, 'Oh, baby, it's beautiful.'

'You doughnut, I'm the surprise!' she said.

I couldn't stop laughing. You couldn't have scripted it. Mind you, she took the Santa outfit off and I've never seen it again, so I never did get to use or keep my surprise!

We have lots of laughs when we are with our mates too. We are really close to our good friends Gary and Phil and also to Nicola, Claire and Neville from our management team. They live nearby and, even though we work together, we spend a good deal of time socialising too; they come over for barbecues with us and we often go to their house for dinner. Claire, Neville and Nicola are an unstoppable management team, I have so much respect for them. Nicola comes to a lot of gigs with me and makes sure no-one takes pictures of me. If my management stop you from doing so, they're not being funny, honest – they are just protecting me, as people have so often sold pictures of Kate and me in the past. If a fan wants a picture taken with me, though, that's not a problem. After all, where would I be without my fans?

Shortly before we spent our second Christmas together we invited Claire, Neville and Nicola, plus Gary, Phil and friends Michelle and Nick over for a pre-Christmas meal. In our dining room there was a beautiful glass and stone table which I wanted to move to the middle of the room, so that we could make it look festive with candles and Christmas decorations. As I began to move it, there was a sickening sound as the glass fell through the table and smashed on to the floor. I couldn't believe it. How on earth was I going to serve dinner to my guests with a giant hole where the table-top should have been?

I rang Claire in a panic, who told me not to worry and to make a table. Make a table? A bit of a tall order! Not easily deterred, however, Phil and I sped over to B & Q to see if we could muster the raw materials needed to make a table in an hour. With our *Blue Peter* heads on, we took two Black and Decker work tables, balanced a piece of plywood between them, covered our construction in a table cloth, and used leftover wedding voiles to cover up any protruding work-table legs. Voila – the perfect dining-room table. From disaster to triumph with a lot of laughs along the way. Our 'table' looked so good we left it there until a new one was bought for us as a belated wedding present.

Kate and I don't wait for that one special day to buy each other gifts; it's something we do all year round. Last Valentine's Day I had a beautiful diamond-encrusted necklace made with the letters K and P (for 'Katie Price' and also 'Katie and Peter'). I had it done in the same style as our wedding symbol and it took two months to make. We always buy each other jewellery. I know she loves her diamonds and she's blinging 100 per cent. I've got to bling at least 50 per cent so that I don't fade out in the background. So I end up buying stuff as well. She bought me my horse Valentine so that I could start learning to ride. She's just waiting for him to get a bit fatter and then he can carry me!

For Kate's birthday in 2005, I whisked her away for a romantic weekend in Venice. We had a spectacular time – we went for gondola rides, we made the most of the gorgeous Italian food and really enjoyed the time together, just the two of us, sun, vino and love. There are few cities more romantic than Venice.

There are so many similarities between me and Kate, it's uncanny. From the day we met I could relate to her immediately. When I see Kate, I honestly see myself five years ago. Since I've been through my breakdown and understood it as a breakthrough, I've come out the other side. Kate, however, is still in that difficult place. I sometimes think I've been sent to help her; I don't mean that to sound like I'm a hero or anything.

Five years ago everything was all about me. Conversations were about me, decisions were about me. I was very self-centred and I wanted to be in control of everything. I wanted to pick which movie we were going to watch, I wanted to choose what we'd have for dinner. It was all about my hair and my lighting being right. You get to a certain stage where you believe your own hype.

I'm very close to my brothers and I've always travelled

with them. They're my life and my best friends. In the beginning they were working with me and then all of a sudden in my mind they started working *for* me. Suddenly I expected Danny to get my bags out of the car. The minute you get to that point, it becomes dangerous.

After a few months of being with Kate I started to notice the whole conversation was always about her. Everything she talked about was about 'her' – her hair, her nails, her clothes, what people are thinking of her. We'd drive somewhere and she'd complain, 'Oh, it's going to be full of people staring at me.' These were the words I used to say and I would almost have a flashback every time I heard them.

We'd often end up having rows. Then I was angry at myself for getting angry at her because I'd think, Hang on, that's what you were like! When people warned me I was heading for a breakdown, I chose to ignore them. I'm scared that she will fall the way I fell.

I first confronted her about it a year ago. I felt that I'd gone all day and all I'd heard Kate talk about was herself. We went to Tesco and she got angry about the woman who *might* approach her. I'd had enough. I said to her, 'Kate, there's more to life than just you.'

Then I remembered that my manager had said exactly the same thing to me five years previously. At the time I was angry with Claire. But here I find myself giving the same advice that I was given. Now I understand why Claire didn't want me to go through the breakdown. But, had I not gone through that experience, I wouldn't be the content person I am today.

I've always written my own songs and had a lot of success

with my music; I had seven top-five hits in Britain and three of those went to number one. I've sold two and a half million copies of my album. I'm not disappointed in my achievements. I'm not so naive as to believe photographers want a picture of me. Kate's the money shot. I'm so proud of her, because I know she has wanted to give it all up so many times. But I hope I'm enough of an encouragement to her. I know where my talents lie now. I'm loving my talent for being a dad.

Kate is an icon, but I don't think she really knows it. There's a sense of paranoia that she could lose it all tomorrow. I thought my breakdown was God's way of saying, 'This is karma for all the bad things you did to girls, the way you treated them.' Now I'm experiencing karma a second time around. I've met Kate at a stage in my life where I've changed so much as a character and a person. Now it's my turn to help Kate and share with her everything I've learned. Because I saw her heading for exactly the same sort of breakdown that I went through. There are times when I almost think that she's me. And I get angry at her the way I used to get angry at myself. She has me, her children, family and a good team around her to protect her.

Sometimes I've found myself attacking Kate the way I was attacked because I don't want her to go through what I went through. I was suicidal. I don't know how I survived. Every day I tried to sleep and sleep so I could get through it and be one step closer to either the end or a miracle. I do think my experience has helped Kate. But I don't believe I've helped make the change; I believe she's helped make her own change. Being content in a situation with her husband and children has shown her a different side of reality. She now knows she has the work side of her life but she also has a family life. I've given her personal security; now she has that, a lot of the pressure has been removed and she has time to think about other things. She is a much more content and settled person now. Yes, sometimes we drive each other crazy, but show me a married couple that don't. The bottom line is that I adore her and she feels the same about me. As long as we have that, we can get through anything.

The world no longer revolves around me and it no longer revolves around her. Instead, in our world, it's all about us.